10/02

:

Special thanks to:
Martina Krueger, for much help and kindness.
Troth Wells and Ian Nixon, for their patience and creativity.
Bart Lienard, for putting up without complaint with endless pleas for help
and much neglect.
My parents Noshirwan and Phyllis, for being lovely.

The No-Nonsense Guide to Climate Change
First published in the UK by
New Internationalist Publications Ltd
Oxford OX4 1BW, UK
www.newint.org

in association with

Verso
6 Meard Street
London
W1F 0EG
www.versobooks.com

Cover photo: The Stock Market

Design by Andrew Kokotka/Ian Nixon, New Internationalist Publications Ltd.
Production editor: Troth Wells

Printed by TJ International Ltd, Padstow, Cornwall, UK.

British Library Cataloguing in Publication Data.
A catalogue record for this book is available from the British Library.

Library of Congress Cataloguing-in-Publication Data.
A catalogue record for this book is available from the Library of Congress.

ISBN - 1 85984 335 2

the **NO-NONSENSE** guide to
CLIMATE CHANGE
Dinyar Godrej

VERSO

Foreword

GLOBAL CLIMATE CHANGE is seen as the biggest threat to the world's environment, with devastating consequences for humans, animals and ecosystems. We are already seeing the first frightening signs of ecosystems under stress, such as the coral reefs, acting as canaries in the coal mine. Indeed, climate change will have consequences for nearly everyone on this planet, and it should therefore be in everyone's interest to get the problem resolved.

Global problems need global cooperation. Unfortunately, despite governments' current attempts at international negotiations to curb emissions, discussions around the details of how emission reduction commitments shall be met have grown very complex, far removed from the average person. At the time of writing this foreword, climate negotiations have broken down anew because countries like the United States, Japan, Canada and Australia refused to change their ways and showed no signs of flexibility.

If we want to avoid dangerous climate change, we will have to change the way in which we produce our energy. Industrialized countries have to invest in sustainable technologies domestically and then assist developing countries through technology transfer towards a path of sustainable energy economy.

The sad reality is that in both industrial and developing countries, investments are being made every day that lock them into old-fashioned fossil-fuel technologies. Every one of these decisions delays the transition to cleaner energy systems and guarantees the input of yet more carbon dioxide into the atmosphere.

Greenpeace believes that it is possible to completely change the way the world provides for its future energy needs. We can no longer assume that fossil fuels will provide the bulk of our energy in the future. Instead, changes need to be made now to move towards a future where our energy needs are met by clean, renewable energy. Greenpeace therefore campaigns for a switch in investments away from fossil fuels and towards renewable energy; and for the removal of institutional, political and market barriers to the mainstreaming of renewable energy.

The task is huge and demands the cooperation of all members of society. The more aware people become of the alarming threats of climate change and the many possible ways to address them – the easier it will be to catalyze change. And this change requires a strong public opinion to stand up against the vested interest of fossil fuel protagonists, who want to steer countries into a 'fossil fuel as usual' society, locking them into unsustainable energy pathways.

To this end, it is important that the public is aware of the risks of climate change to their living conditions as well as of the possible solutions. For only when the public appreciates the dire consequences of non-action as well as the possible pathway towards a sustainable energy future, will we be able to realize true change.

Governments should not merely listen to the big companies that try to influence politics for their own short-term profit interests. Governments have to answer to their people and heed their demands for genuine sustainable development.

Climate change is a pressing problem. But it is not at all an easy subject to tackle because of the complexities of the science and of the politics. Books like *The No-Nonsense Guide to Climate Change* are invaluable tools to spread critical information across a vast section of society. This book is written in a style that engages the reader, drawing them closer into appreciating what used to be a rather boring and incomprehensible discussion of the climate change issue.

Dinyar Godrej demonstrates a keen interest in the issue, has a good sense of what the real priorities are and has avoided the technical terms and jargon that make it so difficult for the lay person to follow this process. The more people understand what is at stake, the more involved they will be. And this involvement means having more citizens acting as watchdogs to the process – making it all the more difficult for governments and companies to betray the global community.

Athena Ronquillo-Ballesteros
Regional Energy Campaigner/Campaigns Co-ordinator
Greenpeace Southeast Asia

the **NO-NONSENSE** guide to
CLIMATE CHANGE

CONTENTS

the **NO-NONSENSE** guide to
CLIMATE CHANGE

I GREW UP with the regular seasons of Central India.
With the annual pulse of the monsoon rains providing
most of the drama, the rest of the year followed a fairly predictable pattern, the weather often changing
little for weeks at a time.

So, even though I had heard about it, I was still
surprised by the degree of variety within the broad
outline of the seasons, when I moved to Northern
Europe over a decade ago. Rain no longer fell at its
assigned time of year, but could turn up on any day at
all, out of the blue, in a matter of hours. Despite my
newfound fascination with the weather, it took a long
time for me to become interested in and engage with
the idea of climate change.

For a start it all seemed so imponderable and vari-
able. We are talking of gigantic natural systems and
their interplay with a web of human activities, of a
bewildering array of contributions from a wide range
of scientific disciplines, of the essential difficulty of
measuring and modeling changes on a global scale for
something as elusive and diverse as the weather systems which make up regional climates. The messages
did not sink in straight away.

Then there was the uncertainty factor. Part of it was
natural incredulity. Looking at the vast arc of the sky
and all the weather omens that lurked within it, I
found it difficult to believe that we human beings
were effecting a destructive change on such a grand
scale. There was also the collection of 'possibles' and
'probables' that accompanies scientific reports on climate change. I began to realize that scientists almost
never say that they are certain, even when they may be

over 90 per cent sure of something.

There was also the immediacy factor. Just as the other big challenges facing the world – poverty, indebtedness and globalization, for example – can seem 'out there' unless connections are made with our own lives or we have firsthand experience of them, so climate change seemed distant, playing out over a time scale of several years.

Finally, there was the 'if-I-ignore-it-maybe-it-will-go-away' factor that seems universal to human experience. It's a kind of inertia to change, especially change of the radical variety, which allows us to keep going as usual, despite all the information to the contrary we may have accepted at a rational level.

Many things happened to make me take climate change seriously. One was realizing that the same kind of short-term self-interest as had spawned a string of other environmental crises was also responsible for climate change. Another was that the destructive potential of major climatic shifts was possibly greater than any other havoc our species had hitherto wreaked on the Earth.

Next, the scientific odds began to make more sense. If I knew that the odds of my being involved in a train crash were 50 per cent, I doubt I would ever set foot in a train again. And yet the probability of climate change is much higher, near certain, so why aren't people fired up by the issue to take immediate action? Over the last decade different strands of scientific research have begun to mesh ever closer, building a solid wall of consensus that is difficult to ignore. All the probabilities are pointing in the same direction. But the final push has been provided by the weather itself, which began throwing up nasty surprises and breaking records with such frequency in the 1990s that it made a wide range of people sit up and take notice. Globally, the 1990s was the warmest decade of the last millennium and 1998 its hottest year.

Senior citizens across the world can remember just how different things were only a half-century ago. Sometimes the time scale for a new pattern to evolve is shorter still. I remember as a child, escaping the ferocity of the central Indian summer for holidays in the 'hill stations' of the lower reaches of the Himalayas. Suddenly instead of letting me run around in a vest and shorts, my mother would bundle me up in sweaters, gloves, scarf and a much-hated hand-knitted woolen cap complete with pompom. I remember my fascination with seeing my breath leave my mouth in a little cloud. I would walk around going 'Hah' just to let it happen.

Nowadays many of these towns are reporting big temperature rises in the summer months and people are investing in electric fans where previously there was no need. Malaria-bearing mosquitoes can now survive in some of the regions previously clear of them. Some vegetables normally grown in these areas are showing a deterioration in quality and yield. It isn't just a question of rising temperatures either: the entire cycle of the region's seasons is showing disruption. All of this in a span of about 30 years.

Today the talk is no longer just that the climate will alter in the future but of the changes happening now, in the present. However this switch in tenses has brought little corresponding change in the behavior that led us to this state of affairs and which will continue to turn the climatic screw. For instance, international climate negotiations aimed at curbing emissions of the gases that are powering global warming have so far resulted in more hot air than firm action. In 1997 representatives of the industrialized countries – responsible for the lion's share of emissions – agreed to a cut of just 5.2 per cent over the emissions levels in 1990, the cut-off year. The reductions needed are actually in the region of 50 to 70 per cent, and even this high estimate has seen upward revisions recently. If the agreement to a 5.2 per cent cut was symptomatic of a lack of real commitment, then the fact that even this low target is nowhere near being reached and that many individual countries are actually increasing emissions year on year after pledging cuts is enough to make the stoutest souls lose hope.

But in the face of the likelihood of more and more extreme weather in our own lifetimes – not two or three generations hence – hope must be created. The changes we are witnessing today are the result of greenhouse gas emissions from over half a century ago when levels were much lower than they are today. Bearing this time-lag in mind we can expect much worse to come. So whilst traditional politics seems more concerned with misguided economic priorities than taking decisive action, the time has come to put the spotlight on a different kind of politics. We have seen people in their thousands take to the streets to protest against the unjust indebtedness of Majority World countries and the tyrannies of the globalization of world trade. It is time to make our voices heard on the climate issue as well and let politicians and big business know that we demand real solutions while these still have a chance of succeeding.

We are living in a world which is growing ecologically poorer every day and whose biodiversity grows ever smaller as a result of human actions. If we allow our species to become the architects of climatic catastrophe, it will not be the end of the world: life on the planet has survived cataclysmic events during the course of at least three billion years before we humans turned up on the scene. Think of the dinosaurs. But our own survival and that of numerous other species could become much harder.

Dinyar Godrej
Rotterdam

1 Overview of climate change

The evidence for climate change... the outlook... how 'feedbacks' could lead to runaway global warming, and the crises facing humanity.

WHEN WE ARE ill with a fever, our body temperature changes from being 'normal' at around 98.1° Fahrenheit (36.7° Celsius) to fever pitch at 98.6° F (37° C). This tiny increase of 0.5° F (0.3° C) switches us from feeling well to feeling sick. This sensitivity of the human body to temperature changes is one way of appreciating the phenomenon of climate change (powered as it is by global warming) which has taken up permanent residence in the world's headlines.

The world's 'normal' temperature from the frozen environs at the poles to the noonday furnaces of some of its deserts evens out at an average of around 57.2° F (14° C). According to Brazilian ecologist and former Minister for the Environment José Lutzenberger, 'The range propitious to life ranges from a few degrees below zero [32° F], where life survives by resting, to about 80° C [176° F] above zero for a few organisms, some bacteria and algae that manage to live in hot springs, which makes a total of about 100° C [180° F].'[1] Lutzenberger makes a comparison with possible temperatures in the universe – from about -459.4° F (-273° C), also known as absolute zero, on the outer planets like Pluto and Neptune to an estimated 10,832° F (6,000° C) on the sun, to hundreds of billions of degrees within supernovas. If this range were to be plotted on a line where every degree corresponded to a fraction of an inch, or a millimeter, it would stretch to hundreds of thousands of miles or kilometers. And of this, the range within which the Earth's creatures survive would account for a mere 4 inches or 10 centimeters.

This humbling calculation is a reminder of the uniqueness of life on our planet. All life forms thrive within this small range of temperatures, in sharp contrast to the wastes of our planetary neighbors. And most life is sensitive to small changes in temperature within this relatively narrow range.

Recently the notion of global warming has taken on an increased urgency because the 1990s have been the warmest decade of the millennium, whilst the 20th century counts as the hottest century. The seven warmest years on record occurred in the 1990s with 1998 shooting so high off the scale that it has earned the dubious distinction of being the hottest year of the millennium. The positive change in temperature over the 20th century reveals it to be in the region of 1.4°F (0.8°C), which may not seem like much, but appears to be operating like the change that triggers a fever.

In fact the change, if one considers the enormity of the forces involved – the great landmasses, the oceans, the lower atmosphere – is not small at all. And in the last two decades in particular, the Earth has been warming at a rate that is faster than at any point in the

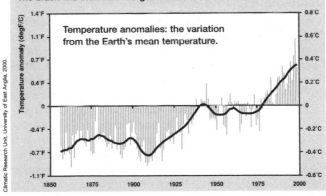

Global air temperature
This time series shows the combined global land and sea surface temperature record from 1856-1999. The 1990s were the warmest decade, with 1998 the warmest year at 0.57°C above the 1961-90 mean.

In the graph, the thin vertical lines represent yearly fluctuations. The black line indicates the general trend. ■

Temperature anomalies: the variation from the Earth's mean temperature.

Climatic Research Unit, University of East Anglia, 2000.

last 1,000 years.

Though all the phenomena that indicate climatic change are wider than global warming, there is little doubt that this is the engine pushing these changes. The reason for this, put very simply, is the fact that the world's weather systems are driven by the sun's energy. Each year the Earth receives energy equivalent to 1,000 trillion (a trillion = a million million) barrels of oil in the form of sunlight.[2] Much of it gets reflected right back into space by the shiny surfaces of snow and ice. The rest functions as a kind of pump driving ocean currents, evaporation, snow and rain. Trees absorb some of this sunlight and release vapor by recycling the water they have taken up from the soil, further fueling the constant movement of life-giving water on our planet. Brazilian physicist Eneas Salati estimates that the energy flow each day over the Amazon Basin alone is comparable to between five and six million atom bombs.[3] But despite these huge, almost unfathomable quantities, the world's weather systems are quite finely tuned entities – knock them and they could tip out of balance. Add more energy into the equation in the form of global warming and there are bound to be corresponding accelerations and imbalances.

Detecting warming

A warming of 1.4° F (0.8° C) in global terms has all the regional variation and complexity that we can expect from, say, the weather in different parts of the world. For one, it has been uneven, with the greatest variations being over land in the middle-to-high latitudes of the northern hemisphere, although localized areas such as the southern Mississippi Valley have actually cooled. Worldwide temperatures have crept up most during nighttime and have made the strongest rises during the northern winter and spring months. The US winter of 1999-2000 was declared the warmest since records began. It was the third time in a row that winter temperature records had been broken. The poles have witnessed freak changes, with some recording stations registering rises of up to 9° F (5° C).

Whilst temperature records go back only for less than 150 years, scientists have been excavating the Earth's temperature going much further back using 'proxy methods', taking measurements from tree rings, deep ice cores, sea sediments and ground bores. What these prehistoric records reveal is staggering – at no point in the last 1,000 years has the Earth's temperature changed as rapidly as in the 20th century.

Tracing the changes

Today the idea that human activities could be fueling this change in temperatures and with it changes in the world's weather has a wide currency. But to arrive at that conclusion one needs to account for other perfectly natural possibilities that can cause the climate to vary.

Over the lifetime of the Earth there can be little doubt that variations in the amount of solar energy given out by the sun have changed climatic systems considerably. If tomorrow the sun's output of energy increased even fractionally, it would result in quite radical climatic changes on Earth. But for the warming observed through the past century, perhaps the most persuasive natural argument was that put forward by Knud Lassen of the Danish Meteorological Institute. He proposed that the 11-year cycle of sunspot activity on the face of the sun seemed to synchronize with trends in global temperatures, a theory which was a particular favorite amongst those who wished to believe that nothing could be done about global warming. But in 2000 Lassen admitted weaknesses in his hypothesis, telling a meeting of the European Geophysical Society that sunspots and solar cycles couldn't explain the dramatic surge in temperatures since 1980. His colleague Peter Thejll said, 'The curves diverge after 1980, and it is a startling deviation. Something else is acting on climate. It has the fingerprints of the greenhouse effect.'

Another theory, posited in the 1920s by Serbian meteorologist Milutin Milankovich, claimed that changes in the tilt and orbit of the Earth over periods spanning millennia could cause climatic changes because they would affect the way the sun's energy was distributed on different parts of the planet. The 100,000-year shift in the Earth's orbit around the sun could, according to Milankovitch, be the underlying cause of our planet's cycles of ice ages. However, Milankovitch's cycles are not enough in themselves to explain the making of ice ages and one has to invoke other factors such as a decrease in atmospheric levels of the greenhouse gas carbon dioxide (see below).

Volcanic explosions also have the capacity to shake the system – cooling the Earth rather than warming it. They throw up vast clouds of dust and sulfur dioxide into the lower atmosphere. The dust eventually settles or gets rained out, but the sulfur dioxide spreads a cloak of pollution, which reduces the amount of the sun's energy that hits the Earth. Volcanic eruptions can cool the Earth's temperatures by about 0.4-0.5°F (0.2-0.3° C). But such effects in the 20th century have rarely lasted for more than a few years, so they cannot be held responsible for changes over the longer term.

The overheated engine of human progress

All of which points to another likely culprit – human influence. The havoc that humans are playing with the weather has ironically the stuff of all life on Earth as its basis. This is the element carbon, the essential building block of anything that breathes or grows, whether animal, vegetable, or in-between. The Earth is packed with it in the form of their remains. But it also envelops the planet in the form of the gas carbon dioxide, invisible but with one remarkable quality that it shares with a few other gases. It allows the sun's energy to reach the Earth's surface relatively unhindered, but traps the amount of energy re-emitted by the warmed Earth (which is of a longer wavelength), before it can escape

The greenhouse effect

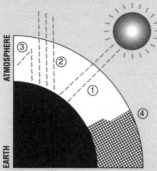

A layer of gases in the atmosphere acts like an insulating blanket trapping solar energy that would otherwise escape into space. Without these 'greenhouse gases' the earth would be frozen, barren and lifeless.

HOW IT WORKS

1. Solar energy enters the atmosphere unaffected by greenhouse gases.

2. The sun's rays are absorbed by the Earth, then reflected back at longer heat wavelengths.

3. Greenhouse gases absorb some of this heat, trapping it within the lower atmosphere.

4. When greenhouse gas concentrations increase, more heat is captured causing temperatures in the lower atmosphere and surface to rise. This affects both weather and climate. ∎

to space. By bringing about this delay it performs the ultimate life-giving function, keeping the world's temperature at an even keel. The dance of carbon in the air is a remarkable one – we exhale it with every breath, it is liberated through volcanic explosions, fires and the decomposition of dead things. And, on the other hand, plants both on land and in the sea draw it back down in order to make their food. They later release some at night when they respire and the rest is liberated when the plants die or are burnt or get eaten by animals which then produce methane. But for the duration of their life cycles – which for some trees can be hundreds of years – they store carbon on Earth. The waters of the oceans – which are the only true sink of carbon dioxide and the only net producers of oxygen – are constantly soaking it up. In fact the carbon stores of the oceans are around 50 times greater than the entire amount of carbon in the atmosphere. It's a system of endless recycling – or at least it should be.

Sadly a vital component of human advancement

since industrialization began, aided by greed, is throwing the system off-balance. By burning fossil fuels (coal, oil and natural gas) to supply our power and manufacturing needs and to drive our cars, we're adding over six billion tons* of carbon to the atmosphere each year – a fraction of the amount already up there, but extra nonetheless, building up year on year. Its levels in the atmosphere could double pre-industrial levels by 2080 (though many commentators fear we may not have to wait that long, some putting the year by which this happens as early as 2030). Alongside this the chopping down of forests continues unabated, diminishing the Earth's ability to soak up carbon. With almost half of the world's forests gone, this is really switching on the heat from both ends.

Climate modeling

The question that has vexed many minds is of the degree of confidence with which we can attribute climate change to such human activities. After all, whatever the human contribution may be it is bound to be 'superimposed on, and to some extent masked by, natural climate fluctuations'.[4] How then to distinguish the human influences, the human signal, from the background noise of natural fluctuations? In order to do this, a change that diverges from the normal range must first be detected and then plausible causes found that can explain that change. The relationship between carbon dioxide and the warming of the Earth's atmosphere is nothing new. Swedish scientist Svante Arrhenius had suggested back in 1896 that increased levels of the gas in the atmosphere would lead to warming. But his theories only got dusted down again when attention started turning towards climate change in the 1980s. At that time climate modeling was being more fully developed with the aid of computers. Climatic modeling is an extremely com-

*1 US ton = 2,000 lbs. 1 metric tonne = 2,240 lbs/1,000 kg.

plex business and yet comparatively lacking in sophistication when compared with the complexity of all the factors that actually contribute to climate. Whereas short-term weather forecasts use satellite and ground data of observable weather phenomena, to give a reasonably accurate short-term prediction, climate modeling looks at the longer term-frame of seasons and years and gives the broad outlines for them. In this it too is reasonably accurate.

In fact the leading body on climate change – the United Nations' Intergovernmental Panel on Climate Change (IPCC) which has input from over 2,000 of the world's leading scientists working in various fields with a bearing on the subject – has been constantly refining models to improve the accuracy of the forecast. The numbers of variables that are fed into such models strain the abilities of even the supercomputers used for this work. And naturally, as the amount of anthropogenic emissions of greenhouse gases in the future could vary depending on whether restrictions are imposed or not, climate models also have to take into account different emissions scenarios and make predictions accordingly.

Rather than basing the analysis on overall warming, the models take into account patterns of change over different geographical regions and over the seasonal variations. This is because the causes of climate change show different patterns of climate response, which the modelers try to match with changes that have already been observed. Confidence in the models was boosted when they were run backwards over the past century and their predictions gave the correct general outline of climatic changes for that period. A climate model also correctly predicted the damping of temperatures and period of recovery after the eruption of Mount Pinatubo in the Philippines in 1991.

The IPCC's findings make for disturbing reading, none more so than the temperature increases that have been forecast, with an increase of up to 5.4°F (3°C) on the cards by 2100 if nothing is done about greenhouse gas emissions. Their forecast had been initially higher, but has been revised downwards, ironically, to account for increases in pollution. We have been pumping aerosols (sulfate particles) into the atmosphere that reflect some of the incoming solar energy and have a cooling influence. If 5.4° F (3° C) doesn't seem like very much, it is worth remembering that a fall of just that magnitude brought on the last ice age.

As carbon dioxide is the biggest player in the climate change stakes, much research has gone into establishing that the increase in the gas is really due to human activity. Fortunately there is a fail-safe way of establishing this. The nuclei of carbon atoms in the

The major greenhouse gases

Without its protective atmosphere the Earth would be 71.2°F (33°C) colder – frozen and lifeless. But over 99 per cent of the atmosphere – composed of nitrogen and oxygen – does not retain much of the sun's heat. The gases that cause the natural greenhouse effect, trapping some of the sun's heat and making life possible form just a tenth of one per cent of the atmosphere's total volume.

Human activities have sent levels of greenhouse gases soaring – concentrations of carbon dioxide, the most important one, could be double pre-industrial levels by 2080 according to the Intergovernmental Panel on Climate Change (IPCC).

• **Carbon dioxide**
Current levels are higher than in the last 200,000 years according to geological records. While nature produces about 30 times more than humans as part of a finely tuned cycle, we still spew over 20 billion tonnes* of the gas each year mainly through the burning of fossil fuels. Land-use changes such as deforestation and clearing of land for logging, ranching

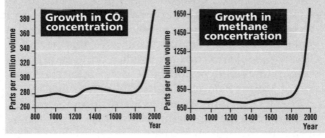

gas in emissions from natural and human processes are different. Naturally released carbon dioxide's carbon atoms have a measurable level of radioactivity. But the nuclei of carbon from fossil fuel sources have lost this radioactivity after being buried deep in the Earth for millions of years. Tree rings have provided the evidence that concentrations of radioactive carbon-14 are getting diluted, which means there is more carbon dioxide from the burning of fossil fuels around.

Scientists have also been measuring the precise amounts of the gas in the atmosphere since the 1950s and they have observed an increase in its levels with each successive year. Ice cores from the Greenland and Antarctic ice caps pro-

Contribution to global warming

- Nitrous oxide 5%
- Other CFCs 8%
- CFC 11 and 12 17%
- Methane 15%
- Carbon dioxide 55%

and agriculture account for 15 to 20 per cent of human emissions. These additional emissions accumulate and could hang around for another 200 years warming the planet.

• **Methane**

Twenty times more powerful than carbon dioxide, methane levels have risen a full 145 per cent above natural levels. This gas is created through deforestation, decomposition of waste, and rice and cattle production and stays around for 12 years. If the permafrost (the part of the Earth's surface in arctic regions that remains permanently frozen) starts melting, large stores of methane could be released.

• **Nitrous oxide**

Heavy use of chemical fertilizers in industrial-style agriculture has increased levels of this gas by 15 per cent. Nitrous oxide is 200 times more powerful than carbon dioxide and stays around for 120 years.

• **Chlorofluorocarbons (CFCs)**

These gases were first manufactured in the 1930s for activities such as refrigeration and air-conditioning. They had myriad uses – such as foam-blowing agents and in aerosol sprays. Their warming effect is thousands of times stronger than carbon dioxide. Although they are being phased out they will linger for several thousand years and there are fears that other fluorocarbons that are being used as substitutes could add to the greenhouse effect in the future. ∎

1 US ton = 2,000 lbs. 1 metric tonne = 2,240 lbs/1,000 kg.

Climate Change: Awareness and Action, Dave Mussell, Juleta Severson-Baker, Tracey Diggins, Pembina Institute for Appropriate Development, Ottawa, 1999; The Ecologist, March/April 1999; UNEP and WMO.

vide a record of the atmosphere going back 200,000 years in the tiny bubbles of air trapped in the ice when it first fell to the ground as snow. These same air bubbles also contain a record of temperatures for long

Northern Europe and the big chill

On the Lofoten islands off the coast of Norway in winter mists rise above the Norwegian sea, bathing the surroundings in an air of dreaminess. Although these islands are within the Arctic Circle they enjoy a much more equable climate than might be expected. The mist hanging over the sea is the reason. It forms because the sea is several degrees warmer than the air above it, causing the moisture in the air to condense. Lofoten owes its inhabitability to the warming presence of the Gulf Stream, an ocean current that keeps temperatures in large parts of Northern Europe far milder than they would otherwise be.

But global warming could have a nasty surprise waiting for this region – far from turning it into some Mediterranean-type haven there is the distinct possibility that the climate here could resemble that of chilly Labrador or even Siberia in the span of a century or two. The reason for this would be the moving southwards of the Gulf Stream due to vast quantities of freshwater melting from the warming North Pole. More dramatically the Gulf Stream could stall and even switch off, causing winter temperatures to plummet by 18°F (10°C) or more. This could happen because the pump of the Gulf Stream works in the freezing waters of the Greenland Sea. As the seawater begins to freeze here, the remaining water becomes denser, with a much higher salt concentration. This colder, saltier water sinks slowly to the ocean floor and begins its tortuous journey to the South Pole, thus pulling warm water from the tropics up towards the north. The Gulf Stream is part of a gigantic conveyor belt of ocean currents that straddles the globe from pole to pole. But if increasing quantities of melt water at the North Pole kept the sea water diluted then it could gradually stop sinking, slowing the pump down, possibly leading to a point where the pump could switch off.

The southward movement of the Gulf Stream could well be upon Northern Europe within the next few decades, with the big chill descending in the span of perhaps two hundred years. Professor Nicholas Owens of the Plymouth-based Public Marine Laboratory put the odds of this happening in a warming world like this, 'I wouldn't like to say which way it will go. But the smart money is on skiwear rather than flip-flops. We will simply get the weather we should have for the latitude at which we live.' ■

'Global Warming to leave UK out in the cold', Mark Rowe, *The Independent on Sunday,* 8 October, 2000; 'How global warming could cause Northern Europe to freeze', Peter Bunyard, *The Ecologist*, March/April 1999.

before direct measurements began. Recently a study of boreholes in the Earth's surface conducted over 616 sites on all continents except Antarctica also confirmed the rise in temperatures this century. This study worked by calculating the rate at which temperatures penetrate downwards from the surface of the Earth.[5]

Today's carbon dioxide levels are 30 per cent above pre-industrial levels and at the rate at which energy demand is growing they could double before the century is out. This is a staggering change when one considers that levels have stayed the same with only slight fluctuations for thousands of years, as revealed by the ice core record. Evidence has also come from the measurements of the gas at different locations on the planet, showing slightly higher readings for the northern hemisphere. As the majority of fossil fuel burning activities are taking place in the North and atmospheric circulation patterns delay the arrival of northern emissions to the southern hemisphere by about a year, the pattern is entirely consistent.

All change

So what's in store? The general predictions of the IPCC scientists include a greater degree of warming over landmasses than over seas, as the darker, rougher surfaces of land soak up solar energy better. The Arctic will see the greatest amount of warming in its winter temperatures. Nighttime warming will be greater than that for daytime. For the mid-latitudes (most of North America, Europe, parts of South America) the number of hot days in summer will increase whilst exceptionally cold days will decrease in number.

The most worrying predictions though concern the unpredictable – there will be an increase in extreme weather events such as freak floods and prolonged droughts and they will last longer. Not all the changes would have to do with warmer weather as such; the increased energy flows could drive more intense blizzards and snowstorms as well. With temperatures rising there will be increased evaporation both from land and sea. The latter could translate into increased rainfall. But this will not be an orderly change, with the rainfall compensating for the drying out of the land. Instead there will be all sorts of local imbalances, some areas turning to desert after their soils have been baked dry whilst others see topsoil washed away by floods. Storms will become more frequent and intense, coastal regions could be awash with rain while great continental interiors dry up.

The most worrying aspect of these changes are that they have been calculated assuming gradual global climate change, but the distant past offers evidence for abrupt switches in climate. And the fear is that climate systems could undergo just such a dramatic flip, from which recovery would be a matter of centuries rather than decades (see box: Northern Europe and the big chill).

Whilst one cannot link any particular extreme weather event with certainty to global warming, the frequency of record-breaking events in each year of the 1990s has made commentators invoke it with frightening regularity.

Feedbacks that could be paybacks

Particularly alarming are the possibilities of indirect effects of this warming that could further accelerate climatic changes. These are known as 'positive feedbacks' and so far they have not been adequately accounted for in the climate models.

With the warming of the oceans and the surface air above them, evaporation would increase, increasing the amount of water vapor in the air. Water vapor is in fact the most potent natural greenhouse gas, and any increase, caused indirectly by warming due to increases in other greenhouse gas concentrations, would further trap heat. Frank Wentz, a physicist at Remote Sensing Systems of Santa Rosa, California, analyzed data from three NASA satellites to come up with the

Extreme weather, 2000

NORTH AMERICA

Boston sets a record for snowless days.

Record ice storm cuts power lines in northern Georgia.

Freak snowstorms in Arkansas, Oklahoma and Texas.

Heavy snowfall then sudden rise in temperatures cause avalanches in Alaska.

Winter 1999-2000 declared warmest on record.

Water levels in the Great Lakes lowest for 35 years.

Fire season sweeps across 11 states by August.

Record drought in Texas, Louisiana and Alabama ruins crops.

CENTRAL AMERICA

Jamaica: Crops affected by drought.

SOUTH AMERICA

Brazil: Thousands homeless after torrential rains. Worst floods in 25 years.

Venezuela: Epidemics of dengue fever and malaria after floods and landslides.

Argentina: Floods in the northwest of the country.

Colombia: Intense rains ruin coffee crop.

Peru: Military called to combat locust swarms.

EUROPE

Heat waves in Turkey, Bulgaria, Romania and Greece.

France: Damage from windstorms estimated at $10 billion.

Czech Republic: Floods.

Norway: A record 6 feet (2 meters) of snow falls in the north.

Hungary: Floods.

Romania: Floods.

Cyprus: Forest fires.

Switzerland: Floods and mudslides destroy villages in the Swiss Alps.

Britain: Widespread flooding, described as the worst in over 50 years.

Sweden: Floods follow weeks of heavy rain.

MIDDLE EAST

Israel: Heaviest snowfall in 50 years.

Iran: Worst drought in more than 30 years.

AFRICA

Kenya: Severe drought for third year. Cattle lost; 4m people affected.

Mozambique: Worst floods in 50 years. 100,000 displaced. Floods in Botswana and South Africa as well.

Ethiopia: Drought continues for fourth season killing 95 per cent of livestock. Widespread famine affects 8 million.

Madagascar: Two cyclones rip through forests.

ASIA

Philippines: Floods leave 20,000 homeless.

Indonesia: National disaster declared after forest fires return. Floods kill hundreds in West Timor.

Mongolia: Nearly 2 million cattle lost to prolonged drought. People affected by famine.

India: Worst drought in 100 years in the northwest affects 50 million; North India suffers intense monsoon leaving 4.5 million homeless; South India gets record rainfall; Severe floods kill 1,200 in the east.

Afghanistan: Worst drought in 30 years. Widespread famine.

China: Flash flood in Gansu province, one of the driest regions in the country; Worst drought in 20 years in Beijing area; Three years of drought turn farmlands in eastern China into a new desert.

Cambodia: Worst floods in 40 years.

Japan: Worst rainfall in 100 years displaces 45,000 people.

Bangladesh: Floods kill several hundreds.

Vietnam: 300 people die in floods.

Tajikistan: Worst drought in 50 years threatens 6 million with famine.

AUSTRALIA

Hit by cyclone; Warm, wet weather causes locust swarms. Floods in New South Wales after drought.

ANTARCTICA

A piece from the Ross ice-shelf the size of Jamaica breaks off due to warming temperatures.

Extreme weather chronology, Ross Gelbspan, environmental journalist, http://www.heatisonline.org/

alarming conclusion that this feedback has already
begun. During the 1990s he found the amount of water
vapor in the atmosphere had gone up by two per cent.[6]

Once positive feedbacks are triggered, they could go
on to trigger others, leading to runaway warming – the
models may not predict it but that it is possible cannot
be denied. Here is a hypothetical but not entirely
improbable doomsday scenario. As greenhouse gases
build up in the atmosphere, temperatures rise. Forests
begin to dry and die back or burn. Felling continues
apace, diminishing forests' ability to draw down carbon
dioxide. Areas under ice melt to expose the Earth
below, which begins to soak up the sun's heat instead
of reflecting it. Long-frozen tundra-vegetation begins
to decompose releasing more carbon dioxide and
methane. The seas, swollen by rising temperatures and
melting polar ice, swallow densely populated coastal
regions. With warming they also begin to lose their
ability to absorb carbon dioxide and could start releasing the gas already dissolved in them – estimated at 50
times the amount contained in the atmosphere... and
so on. As vicious circles go this one is hard to beat.

As the 20th century closed, the warming speeded
up, with average global temperatures jumping by half
a degree Celsius (0.9° F) in the last 25 years. This
would be the equivalent of 2° C or 3.6° F per century.
However the amount of change to which ecosystems
can adapt is estimated at a maximum of 1° C (1.8° F)
over a century. And that is if no further changes are
expected. But as Thomas Karl, director of the National
Climate Data Center – part of the National Oceanic
and Atmospheric Administration (NOAA) in the US –
put it, 'We are already experiencing the rate of warming predicted right through this coming century.'[6]
And there could be worse to come as today's effects
are believed to be mainly the work of carbon dioxide
emitted half a century ago. The much higher levels of
emissions today are damage we are storing up for the
future. Also to be factored into the equation are the

effects of sulfate aerosols, by-products of industrial pollution which have masked the greenhouse effect by their cooling properties. But they have a short atmospheric lifetime and as cleaner production processes become more desirable in our increasingly polluted world, their role could well decline, revealing the true extent of warming.

Carbon store

With temperatures in the high latitudes rising the most rapidly not only is the temperature record of the various layers of ice being lost as newly fallen snow often melts completely in the spring thaw, but there is the possibility that vegetation covered by permafrost in the northern hemisphere since the time when dinosaurs roamed the much warmer Earth could be laid bare. This decomposing matter forms a carbon store estimated at as much as 450 billion tonnes*, which could release enormous quantities of carbon dioxide and methane into the atmosphere.

The attack on the world's forests has left us with just a third of the land functioning as an intact forest ecosystem than was once under forest cover. Trees store carbon and draw it down to produce food, but dead, burnt or cleared forests turn from being carbon sinks to carbon sources. Two and a half acres (one hectare) of tropical rainforest contains between 100 and 250 tonnes of carbon in the form of organic matter (a figure which is much higher if one includes the carbon stored in the soil), three-quarters of which could be liberated by burning or decomposition.[3]

With such forests disappearing at the rate of one per cent a year throughout the 1990s and countries often being forced to exploit the economic potential of their timber to service their international debts the outlook is less than bright. Ten long years of discussions with Western governments have led to an

*1 US ton = 2,000 lbs. 1 metric tonne = 2,240 lbs/1,000 kg.

agreement by Brazil to preserve just 10 per cent of the Brazilian Amazon rainforest, the largest in the world, in return for funds from the World Bank's Global Environment Facility – even though the Brazilian Government is relatively enlightened when it comes to climate issues and the rainforest.[7] The Amazon rainforest has often been called the lungs of the Earth because of its circulation of oxygen and its function as a pump for energy released through transpiration which leads to rain-bearing clouds that benefit areas as far-flung as Northern Europe and Scandinavia. The feedback mechanism from rainforest destruction would not only directly impact on warming but could also result in a decline in rainfall in these areas.

Another potential feedback is the release of methane from methane hydrates. These resemble ice in that they are solid, but they are actually an unstable mixture of water and methane forming at low temperatures under considerable water pressure in the oceans. An essential factor for their formation is the presence of a thick enough layer of sediments to generate the methane in the first place. Released from the ocean's pressure they sizzle and disappear into the air in a matter of seconds. The US Geological Survey estimates that the total carbon lurking in methane hydrate deposits is around 10,000 billion tonnes, most of it too far below the ocean's surface to be released. But in the Arctic with its colder water temperatures, less pressure is required for the hydrates to form and as a result they occur in much shallower waters and could conceivably be destabilized if the water warms enough.

As author, earth scientist and solar energy advocate Jeremy Leggett puts it, 'The question is, how much hydrate lies around the Arctic? We do not know for sure, but it must be measured in many tens of if not hundreds of billions of tonnes. And since there is a mere five billion tonnes of carbon in today's stock of atmospheric methane, only a little methane hydrate would need to be melted to boost the greenhouse effect significantly.'[8]

It is just such considerations that don't figure in climate models, but the potential they have to start a chain of runaway feedbacks, however distant it may appear, needs to be acknowledged. And as long as that potential remains we need to act, because once the juggernaut starts rolling it is too late to stop it. This is known as the 'precautionary principle' in the climate debate and the time to apply it is now. For with each bit of corroborative evidence to support global warming, the outline becomes clearer. Waiting for the picture to be complete would be waiting helplessly for catastrophe. This section has dealt with only a few of the possible feedbacks. But the warning signs are there for anybody to see.

The big melt

In March 2000 the Worldwatch Institute in Washington sent out an urgent message that the Earth's ice cover was melting at a far speedier rate than previously predicted: a clear signal that greenhouse gases were heating up the planet.

As this big melt becomes a reality, thoughts turn to the fears of rising sea levels which have beset many small island nations and low-lying coastal regions. The British Meteorological Office's Hadley Center for Climate Prediction and Research, a leading establishment in the field of climate modeling, forecasts an almost 16-inch (40 centimeters) rise in sea waters by 2080 if nothing is done about greenhouse gas emissions. This would mean that annual floods could threaten an estimated 94 million people – up from the 13 million at present. The coastal regions of southern and Southeast Asia would be the worst affected, as storm surges could push sea water deep inland.[9]

For about 40 low-lying island nations worldwide the combination of fiercer storms and sea-level rise could spell complete disaster. Already the United Nations Environment Program (UNEP) has recommended the evacuation of Tarawa atoll, part of the Pacific island nation of Kiribati. Some small islands fringing Kiribati have disappeared under the waters. Roads have had to be moved inland on the main island as the ocean gnaws into the shore. In June 2000 New Zealand (Aotearoa) made a promise of sanctuary to inhabitants of Tuvalu if their coral-atoll sank under the sea. These are the canaries in global warming's coalmine. Yet the sea-level rise that threatens them and which figures in the Hadley Center's predictions is due by and large to the thermal expansion of the warmer seawaters. Now account also needs to be taken of the vast volumes of water that could be released from the world's large ice masses.

The Antarctic peninsula has reported a sustained warming as high as 4.5° F (2.5° C). In places scientists have observed that rocks that have been covered by ice for millennia have begun to poke through. In the mid-1990s a roughly 5,000 square-mile (8,000 square kilometers) ice-shelf, Larsen A, broke away into the sea, looking – as an observing scientist put it – 'like bits of polystyrene foam smashed by a child.'

According to the Worldwatch Institute report, the ice sheet that covers the Arctic Ocean has lost 40 per cent of its volume over the last 30 years and could be completely gone in a matter of decades. This wouldn't make sea levels rise as the ice lies upon water to begin with. But the loss of land-based ice is another story. The Arctic's Greenland ice sheet has had more than 3 feet (1 meter) shaved off it each year since 1993 along its southern and eastern edge.

In Antarctica, three great ice sheets have gone completely, but whether land ice is also melting as rapidly is a matter of dispute. Some studies have suggested that the smaller of the continent's two land ice sheets (with a mass the size of Mexico) is melting faster than normal. If the West Antarctic ice sheet were to collapse, the seas would surge by a catastrophic 18 feet or 6 meters.[10] To put this into perspective, it is estimated that a 3-foot or 1-meter rise in sea level could flood many of the world's major coastal cities, such as New York, London and Bangkok and swallow up three per cent of total land area. Significantly, 30 per cent of the world's croplands could be lost.[11]

In the Netherlands, the famous sea defenses would no longer be able to protect large areas that are under sea level. In April 2000 the inhabitants of the coastal village of Bergen aan Zee were told that the authorities could no longer guarantee their safety due to rises in sea levels. The village, whose name in English can read as 'Bergen on Sea', could become 'Bergen *in* Sea'. Cities like Amsterdam and Rotterdam could follow suit in the event of larger rises.

And it's not just sea ice that is melting – all over the world glaciers are in retreat as well, because the summer melt is more than can be replenished. The Quelccaya glacier in Peru is retreating 10 times faster than a decade ago, threatening water supplies for Lima's 10 million people.

Himalayan glaciers are, according to a UN study, 'receding faster than in any part of the world'. If the Worldwatch report's prediction of shrinkage by a fifth in this region in the next 35 years appears alarmist to some, the UN study is even starker, threatening the complete disappearance of these glaciers in the same time frame. As environmental journalist Fred Pearce put it 'Their eventual disappearance is a potential catastrophe for the hundreds of millions of people in southern Asia, who depend on the summer melt even more than the monsoon rains to irrigate their crops and provide drinking water.'[12]

For the 6,000 people whose lives are at risk from the brimming Tsho Rolpa glacial lake in Nepal, the situation is more urgent. Dozens of such lakes have formed high in the Himalayas in recent history, with only the debris left behind by retreating glaciers damming them in. About every three years, one bursts sending a wall of water rushing down the valleys. For the villagers in striking distance of Tsho Rolpa, every summer since 1994 when the alarm was first sounded has been a tense one. Work is underway to try and siphon out some of the water, but until the situation becomes safer a warning siren triggered by sensors is the only defense the villagers have. It would give them a few precious minutes' notice that the deluge was on its way.

Looking for refuge

In Bangladesh there is a widespread acceptance that seasonal floods are worsening and people have built raised fields with freshwater ponds stocked with fish to help them sit out floods. But such preparedness begs a vital question: with Bangladesh's fertile coastal plains at risk of sinking under the sea by the end of the century, who and what will feed the dispossessed people? Already the number of environmental refugees worldwide has been estimated at 25 million, more than the total of all other refugees. Fleeing into adjoining lands they are largely invisible to the rich West.

The UK charity Christian Aid is calling these events unnatural disasters, because they believe there is nothing natural about them, with climate change at their root. These are staggering events like the October 1999 super cyclone that hit Orissa in India killing 30,000 and displacing 10 million others, or the failure of the rains for the fourth consecutive year in the Horn of Africa in the summer of 2000 which put 16 million people at risk of starvation.

'Nine out of the past eleven disasters to which we have responded have been caused by extreme weather conditions. Country after country is being decimated by these so-called natural disasters,' said Malcolm Rogers, Christian Aid's head of policy. 'The terrible irony is that the poorest countries are suffering, and we believe that this is because of pollution by the wealthiest.' People in industrialized countries generate over 62 times more carbon dioxide pollution per person than people in the least industrialized countries.

The International Federation of Red Cross and Red Crescent Societies has also been pointing out in recent editions of its annual *World Disasters Report* how the fall-out from climate change has been disproportionate in the developing Majority World where people are often living on marginal lands and struggling against great economic odds to eke out a living. The 1999 edition stated that 96 per cent of all deaths from natural disasters happen in developing countries. In the period 1987 to 1996, 44 per cent of all recorded floods were in Asia, yet they caused 93 per cent of all deaths.

When 1997-98's supercharged El Niño phenomenon carved out a path of destruction across the globe, it claimed 21,000 lives as a result of floods, forest fires, droughts and disease. Most of these people lived in developing countries. Whilst weather instability can hit any part of the world, poorer countries often have few defenses and count their losses in lives rather than insurance.

Sometimes protective measures can be far beyond the means of the poor. The cost of protecting a wealthy nation such as the Netherlands from a 20-inch (50 centimeters) rise in sea levels has been calculated at an astronomical $3.5 trillion, though an early report had suggested that it would be cheaper for the country to adapt than to mitigate climate change. For the Maldives, already facing danger from the sea, the costs

El Niño

El Niño is a series of weather disturbances that typically cause storms and flooding over the Pacific coast of the Americas, while Southeast Asia and the western Pacific region suffer drought. The disturbances get their name from the Spanish for 'the Christ child', which is how Peruvian fishers named the phenomenon as it usually peaks around Christmas. The phenomenon is caused by a change in sea-surface temperatures and of atmospheric pressure – during the 1997-1998 El Niño, sea temperatures were up to 9°F (5°C) higher than normal – in the tropical Pacific Ocean region. The onset of an El Niño is usually first observed when warmer waters off the coast of Peru lead to a sharp decrease in the anchovy catch. ∎

are real. The cost of protecting their shorelines currently runs at over $4,000 per foot ($13,000 per meter) of coast.[13]

The series of weather disturbances known as El Niño occur every three to seven years and have always trailed disaster in their wake. But commentators argue that with climate change manifesting itself in more severe weather events, it is also blowing up the manifestations of the El Niño effects. There is also the possibility that an overheated world climate system could result in El Niños returning within much shorter time scales.

The destruction that El Niño brings can be further amplified by ecological damage and poverty, as was the case when Hurricane Mitch hit Honduras and Nicaragua at the tail end of October 1998, killing some 11,000 people. Negotiators at the climate negotiations going on at the time in Buenos Aires observed a minute's silence. Mitch had been downgraded from a hurricane to a tropical storm when it hit Honduras. But with winds forced to rise by mountain ranges, it dropped a year's rainfall in just two days. In its path were flimsy homes crowded onto marginal lands that had been stripped of any vegetation that could have held soil together. They were soon buried under the

Hurricane force

Weather instability can hit any part of the world – but already vulnerable areas are in the greatest danger. Ninety-six per cent of all deaths from natural disasters happen in developing countries. People living in insecure housing on marginal land are the most at risk. ■

RICH WORLD	POOR WORLD
Hurricane Andrew (August 1992) US	**Hurricane Mitch (October 1998) Nicaragua and Honduras**
Losses: **$22 billion**	Losses: **$7 billion**
Amount covered by insurance: **$16 billion**	Amount covered by insurance: **$150 million**
Death toll: **52**	Death toll: **over 11,000**

million or so landslides that occurred. For heavily indebted Honduras, the damage in money terms was equal to 60 per cent of its annual gross domestic product. 'We lost in 72 hours what we have taken more than 50 years to build,' said the Honduran President. The same year China suffered one of the worst floods in its history when the Yangste River basin became inundated. The damage, estimated at $30 billion, was enough to lower the overall growth rate of this vast country.

When insurance giants tremble

Proof of the increasing violence of the world's weather is also coming from the growing jitteriness of the world's insurance giants who are getting more vocal on the issue of climate change, with representatives sharing public platforms with activist groups like Greenpeace. The industry has also made links with the United Nations Environment Program (UNEP).

Assessments by Munich Re, one of the world's largest insurance companies, show natural disasters doubling in frequency every decade in recent years. Of course insurance remains largely a luxury of the rich nations, but with billion-dollar catastrophes turning up with alarming regularity in the 1990s there is concern that future extreme weather events could bankrupt the industry and destabilize world markets. In the US, catastrophe-related losses had grown from about $100 million a year in the 1950s to $6 billion per year in the 1990s. In 1992 Hurricane Andrew drove 11 insurance companies to bankruptcy despite missing vulnerable Miami. One night's fury left a tenth of the insurance industry's global reserves exhausted and resulted in new laws governing the sale of insurance in Florida. There were consequences in the Caribbean too with companies withdrawing or refusing cover against hurricanes. When the world's leaders met to debate emissions curbs on greenhouse gases at a climate conference in Kyoto in 1997, the insurance industry submitted that 'while the effect of climate change on the frequency or severity of extreme weather events remains unknown, it is clear that even small changes in regional storm patterns or in the hydrological cycle could lead to increased property damage.' They warned that changes in the spread of diseases that could occur with climate change could affect the sale of life insurance and pensions.

Ultimately no amount of insurance could shore up those trapped in the midst of catastrophe and if climate change enters a vortex of ever-increasing destructiveness, then democratic political institutions could crumble along with national infrastructures. It would be too late then to cry wolf – that is why it is so essential that we do so now.

The chapters that follow examine some of the potential and real impacts of climate change, the political impasse that is preventing decisive action on the issue and some solutions for our planet. But first, we take a look at that headline-grabber – the ozone hole.

1 'Gaia's fever', José Lutzenberger, *The Ecologist*, March/April 1999.
2 *Climate Change: Awareness and Action,* Dave Mussell, Juleta Severson-Baker and Tracey Diggins, Pembina Institute for Appropriate Development, Ottawa 1999. **3** 'Eradicating Amazon rainforests will wreak havoc on climate', Peter Bunyard, *The Ecologist*, March/April 1999.
4 'Are human activities contributing to climate change?', UNEP and WMO, http://www.gcrio.org/ipcc/qa/0.3.html **5** 'The hole record', Jonathon P Overpeck, *Nature*, 17 February, 2000. **6** *The Cutting Edge*, World Wildlife Fund, March 2000. **7** 'Going, going...', Fred Pearce, *New Scientist*, 10 June, 2000. **8** *The Carbon War*, Jeremy Leggett, Penguin, London 1999. **9** 'Climate change and its impacts: Stabilization of carbon dioxide in the atmosphere', The Hadley Center for Climate Prediction and Research, October 1999. **10** 'Melting of Earth's ice cover reaches new high', Lisa Mastny, Worldwatch News Brief, 6 March, 2000. **11** 'The threat of rising seas', Grover Foley, *The Ecologist*, March/April 1999.
12 'Meltdown in the mountains', Fred Pearce, *The Independent*, 31 March, 2000. **13** *World Disasters Report 1999,* International Federation of Red Cross and Red Crescent Societies, Geneva 1999.

2 The role of ozone

A contradictory gas… how the ozone hole affects our health… measures to protect the ozone layer, and how global warming is making things worse.

THE INHABITANTS OF Punta Arenas in Chile became prisoners in their own homes in October 2000. They weren't hemmed in by insurrection or the threat of infectious disease but by the sun blazing above them. A month earlier NASA scientists had announced the largest ever hole in the ozone layer above Antarctica, over an area more than three times the size of the US. By October it had extended over the tips of Chile and Argentina, opening up over Punta Arenas. As harmful Ultraviolet-B (UV-B) radiation spread over their city, those venturing out during daylight hours risked irreversible damage to their skin and eyes, which could result in cancer and cataracts. In neighboring Argentina, citizens of Ushuaia were warned that unprotected skin could burn after just seven minutes' exposure. The filter of ozone high up in the stratosphere had been whisked off and the ultraviolet radiation was pouring in through the hole, a bit like a beam of light falling through a magnifying lens.

What's eating the ozone layer

Concern about ozone has been around since the 1970s when it was revealed that certain chemicals being used in manufactured products and agriculture could eventually start eating into stratospheric ozone 15 miles (25 kilometers) above the Earth's surface. These included chlorofluorocarbons (CFCs) and other chlorinated substances used in aerosol sprays, refrigeration and air conditioning units, and types of artificial foam. Bromine atoms, released by halons (used in fire-extinguishing equipment), and methyl bromide (a pesticide) have the same effect. However,

the destruction of ozone is not entirely due to manufactured compounds. For example, chloromethane –
which also eats away at ozone – originates from forest
fires and rotting wood. Other compounds such as
nitrogen oxides are implicated too, but the chief
agents of the damage after a series of complex interactions in the atmosphere are chlorine and bromine.
One free atom of chlorine in the stratosphere is capable of destroying as many as 100,000 molecules of
ozone.[1] Such destruction is not permanent, as ozone is
constantly forming by the action of intense sunlight
over the Equator. But extensive damage to the ozone
layer – its thinning in many places and yawning 'holes'
opening up – is not something that gets repaired in a
matter of a year or two. The ozone hole is a seasonal
phenomenon; it closes over in the winter months. But

The ozone hole's effect on health

The persistence – and growth – of the ozone hole at the poles each
spring, despite the reduction in the use of CFCs, points to the lingering
after-effects of these chemicals. The peak of the damage may well be yet
to come. Whilst presenting market opportunities for manufacturers of sun
block and sunglasses, this is really bad news for the rest of us.

One of the impacts of increased Ultraviolet-B (UV-B) radiation is an
increased susceptibility of the immune system, reducing natural
defenses against infectious and fungal diseases. In areas where malnutrition and infectious disease is already widespread, the effectiveness
of vaccines could be reduced. Cataracts are more prevalent among old
and malnourished people in poor countries and this prevalence would
rise with increased exposure to UV-B radiation.

By far the most common connection in the public mind between
human health and the ozone hole is that of the increased incidence of
skin cancers, especially amongst fair-skinned people. Whereas just one
generation ago young children in New Zealand (Aotearoa) would be
encouraged to go out and play in the sunshine and get a 'healthy'
bronzed look, now school teachers will not allow them out to play without a protective layer of sunblock and wide-brimmed headgear.

When UV-B radiation is absorbed by living cells, essential molecules
get damaged including DNA which keeps the cell functioning properly. In
human beings, apart from impairment of the immune response and
cataracts, exposure to UV-B radiation brings with it sunburn, aging skin
and skin cancer.

as long as ozone-destroying substances linger in the atmosphere it will reappear each year.

Contradictions

Ozone behaves in quite contradictory ways and, although widely studied, its contribution to climate change is an area that still has many uncertainties. At the lower atmospheric level, the troposphere, where ozone is a byproduct of traffic pollution, it acts like a greenhouse gas, trapping heat in. But in the stratosphere it actually has a cooling effect, which is lessened when holes appear. Even though estimates are difficult and can change because of seasonal variations in cover, the UN Environment Program (UNEP) reckons that currently the greenhouse effect from tropospheric ozone is more than twice that of the cooling

In the Netherlands, for example, skin cancers are amongst the most common forms of cancer. Despite public education campaigns and being in a temperate zone, the cultural approval for tanning is very widespread. With the first few days of spring sunshine, the sun-worshippers are out in force on the nation's beaches and during the summer vacations many opt for outdoor holidays in warmer climes. Upon returning to work, holiday tans are immediately assessed by colleagues. In Australia the incidence of skin cancer is the highest in the world, despite a greater public awareness of the dangers of the sun's rays. But Australia suffers by its proximity to the Antarctic ozone hole and its sunny climate. For its fair-skinned inhabitants (the majority of Australians) exposure can occur not necessarily due to choice but during relatively short unguarded spells.

The outlook for both countries is not favorable – skin cancers manifest themselves after cumulative exposure, that's why they are commonest amongst the elderly. It is predicted that with the damage to the ozone layer peaking right now, the consequent peak in skin cancers can be expected by 2050. Of course future rises in skin cancer rates will depend on factors that are complex to model such as the extent of ozone depletion, changes in behavior regarding exposure and the age of the population, but one study says non-melanoma skin cancers could rise by up to 50 per cent in the Netherlands and 140 per cent in Australia by 2050. ■

Health and Climate Change, Pim Martens, Earthscan, London 1998.

effect of stratospheric ozone[2] though this range could vary widely. Ozone is contradictory in other ways as well, because whereas up in the stratosphere it actually safeguards the health of living creatures by screening out UV-B radiation, at the tropospheric level it contributes to respiratory disorders.

When action was first mooted to limit the production of the manufactured chemicals that were harming the ozone layer, producers of products like aerosol sprays were incredulous that chlorine could eventually float up as high as 15 miles (25 kilometers). The evidence, decades later, has left little of that incredulity around. As CFCs were considered quite innocuous before their effects became known, their production rocketed – from 75,000 tonnes* in 1954 to up to 800,000 tonnes in 1974. Concentrations are five times as much since then and the bad news is that CFCs could stay around in the atmosphere for thousands of years. Chlorine in the stratosphere should not exceed two parts per billion in order to prevent further damage to the ozone layer. Today it is at least three times over that limit.

Besides cancers and cataracts in humans and other animals, UV-B radiation can also lead to plankton

*1 US ton = 2,000 lbs. 1 metric tonne = 2,240 lbs/1,000 kg.

Getting rid of the ozone-eaters

In the figures below, the first date in each column refers to an agreed *freeze in consumption*. The second is the date of *total phase-out* of the substances. ■

Ozone-depleting substance	Industrialized countries	Industrializing countries
Halon	1992/1994	2002/2010
Chlorofluorocarbons	– /1996	– /2010
Carbon tetrachloride	– /1996	– /2010
Methyl chloroform	1993/1996	2003/2015
Methyl bromide	1995/2005	2002/2015
Hydrochlorofluorocarbons (HCFCs)	1996/2030	2016/2040

The 9th Meeting of the Parties, Montreal, September 1997.

losses in clear seas, reducing their ability to remove carbon dioxide from the atmosphere (so spurring-on global warming) and adversely affecting the marine food chain. Excessive exposure can lead to plant stunting and genetic mutations in some crops like corn. UNEP has found that damage to DNA in plants due to each consequent drop in ozone levels can be disproportionately large.[3] Recent studies are also accumulating evidence that increases in Ultraviolet-B radiation could alter the ways in which plants, animals and microbes interact in nature by causing chemical changes in plant foliage.

The polar regions, where ozone depletion is at its strongest in springtime, thankfully have little human habitation. But thinning ozone beyond the poles increases the risk of skin cancer especially when coupled with fair skins that offer little natural protection against harmful UV-B. According to UNEP a sustained one-per-cent decrease in stratospheric ozone would result in a two-per-cent increase in skin cancers.

Negotiating a solution?

Talks for controlling ozone-depleting chemicals were started in mid-1980 and by March 1985, governments committed themselves to the Vienna Convention for the Protection of the Ozone Layer. The latter year was when the British Antarctic Survey first reported the ozone hole, which sped up negotiations considerably. A Protocol for reductions of ozone-depleting substances was agreed in Montreal in 1987, subsequently revised in the London and Copenhagen amendments with phase-out dates brought forward and more chemicals added to the list of controlled substances. But soon after the Protocol had been agreed upon, scientific evidence showed its provisions to be inadequate and provided the prompt to further action. A schedule for the complete phasing out of ozone-depleting substances was agreed upon in 1997 – record time for global diplomacy. Even though some sources claim the consumption of the major ozone-depletors has fallen by 80 per cent, it is by no means a figure that is uncontested and illicit trade in CFCs is estimated at 25,000 tonnes a year.[4]

Successes in the fight to make good the damage to the ozone layer must be viewed cautiously, as the damage is peaking at the present time and scientists predict that it will be decades before the seasonal ozone hole will cease from appearing. The political fallout from the fight also requires cautious inspection. As Kennedy Graham, director of the Project for the Planetary Interest, writes: 'There is also a degree of skepticism over the extent to which enlightened governmental leadership forged the way to success of the ozone regime, as compared with a dawning recognition of commercial advantage on the part of the manufacturers during the critical period of the late 1980s. Once the technical and financial viability of alternative technologies was discerned, opposition from the private sector diminished and governments found new space in which to negotiate. Thus, it is sometimes contended, it has yet to be demonstrated that humanity is capable of turning away from future global disaster when compelling corporate interests are in favor of 'business-as-usual'.'[4]

There are also questions as to whether the scale of the effort to provide the necessary transfer of ozone-friendlier technologies to the countries of the South is adequate. The transfer of technology is being funded by a Multilateral Fund, into which Northern countries pay in their contributions. But whether this is enough is open to question, as Argentinean parliamentarian Dante Caputo points out: 'They comprise 15 per cent of the global population, consume over 80 per cent of the planet's resources, consume nearly 85 per cent of the ozone-depleting substances, and have sold nearly $30 billion of such substances over the past decade. Is $500 million enough to remedy this?'[5]

With the ozone hole over Antarctica and the severe

depletion over the North Pole showing no sign of improving, an alarming feedback is coming into play – the agent is, once again, global warming. Taking a very visible role are some extraordinary clouds that are appearing at stratospheric levels at the poles. One witness described them over Swedish Samiland – 'As the Sun dips over the horizon, a mass of tear-shaped clouds appears. They are petrol blue and green, and rimmed with vibrant pink – lurid colors that have no business in a sunset. Against the monochrome backdrop of snow and forest, they are shocking.'[6]

These polar clouds owe their origin to the cooling of the stratosphere and have come about, curiously enough, as a result of global warming. As the lower atmosphere warms, the stratosphere registers a corresponding cooling. As temperatures drop to their lowest during the sunless polar winters, tiny traces of moisture in the dry stratosphere get shaped into clouds. Congregating within the clouds are chlorine compounds derived from CFCs. With the arrival of the spring sun these compounds get the solar trigger, unleashing the unstable form of free chlorine, which then proceeds to eat its way through the mantle of ozone during the polar summer. Bromine from halons and methyl bromide works in a similarly destructive fashion.

It is just such previously unheard of interactions, marvelous in their synergy and frightening in their consequences, which are the stuff of global warming.

1 All ozone statistics, unless otherwise indicated, are from *The Breakdown of Climate*, Peter Bunyard, Floris Books, Edinburgh 1999 and 'How Ozone Depletion Increases Global Warming', Peter Bunyard, *The Ecologist*, March/April 1999. **2** See http://www.gcrio.org/ipcc/qa/0.4.html **3** 'Environmental effects of ozone depletion: Interim summary', UNEP, September 1999, http://www.gcrio.org/ozone/unep1999summary.html **4** 'Ozone protection: Introduction', Kennedy Graham in *The Planetary Interest* edited by Kennedy Graham, UCL Press, London 1999. **5** 'Ozone protection: Argentina', Dante Caputo, in *The Planetary Interest* edited by Kennedy Graham, UCL Press, London 1999. **6** 'The hole story', Gabrielle Walker, *New Scientist*, 25 March, 2000.

3 Impacts: human health

Changes in the spread of disease... a field day for vectors... the unequal battle against ill-health... and how epidemics are already being fueled by weather extremes.

IN CENTRAL INDIA where I grew up, the temperature has hovered for days between 104° and 115°F (mid-40s°C) in recent summers. While everyone waits for relief from the monsoon rains, people suffer and even die from the heat. This is at its fiercest during the afternoon, with the deadly dusty *loo* wind blowing down the streets. My memory of this seasonal wind is that it would suck moisture right out of the body, drying sweat in an instant, leaving a film of salt on the skin. Anyone who was not compelled to go outside stayed indoors, preferably with curtains drawn and the fan on. A heat shimmer would rise from roads and any stone surface. In the evening the air would slowly begin to cool but the walls and floors of the house that had been soaking up heat all day long would begin to release it. People would sprinkle water on floors and verandahs. But the current heat waves are in a league of their own and I feel relieved that I no longer have to experience them. Heat waves are becoming commoner in other parts of the world as well – from the US Midwest to Turkey and Romania in 2000 – often shortening the lives of the weakest.

The human body is conditioned to patterns of work and rest – overwork or uninterrupted rest are both likely to make us sick. But when just coping with heat becomes a major task for the body, respite becomes increasingly essential to recharge our batteries. As the atmosphere heats up bringing with it stronger heat waves, nighttime cooling becomes essential. Unfortunately atmospheric heating is not uniform and the biggest rises in temperatures are being measured at night (as also in latitudes higher than 50 degrees). In some places deaths related to heat waves are set to double as early as 2020, and in urban areas the prolonged heat can be expected to bring clouds of smog and allergens, resulting in respiratory problems.

But heat waves are only a small part of the picture in a warming world. Instability in weather patterns is a marked indicator of warming. In some cases this instability manifests itself as extreme changeability, and in others in the form of more prolonged and intense droughts and downpours. Such disasters not only rack up the death toll by themselves as people get swept away or starve, but they also provide springboards for waves of infectious diseases which, once entrenched, defy eradication. In many cases the aftermath of environmental catastrophe in the developing world is a concentration of displaced people living penned in camps with little access to safe water and sanitation. Trying to control outbreaks of diseases in such cases is a bit like attempting to put out wildfires with buckets of water.

Diseases conquer new ground

However, such threats to human life get little coverage in the Western media, which usually contents itself with occasional rumbles of concern over whether malaria will invade Europe. In the middle of what should be autumn, my sleep is still plagued at night by mosquitoes that are hanging around longer than usual as temperatures refuse to dip far enough. Certainly the risk of malaria transmission is doubled over the coming 20 years for most of Southern and Central Europe if one only goes by predicted temperature changes. However, that is to overlook the sophisticated monitoring and eradication capacities of the wealthy nations in this region. Another story of how mosquito-borne disease is already emerging at higher altitudes in the Majority World due to changing temperatures hardly gets told.

In September 1999, front pages showed helicopters

spraying New York with the pesticide malathion as a response to an outbreak of what was first thought to be St Louis Encephalitis, but turned out to be the West Nile virus. Here was a story that seemed to fit the bill: an 'alien' disease striking at the heart of a grand metropolis and the heroic response to it by the world's wealthiest nation. The link between this mosquito-borne disease and that July's heat wave was easy for most people to make. The sequence of events leading up to the outbreak had started much earlier though, with a mild winter that allowed more mosquitoes to survive than was usual and a dry springtime which killed predatory insects and concentrated water pools with organic matter, making for rich breeding grounds. The July heat wave provided the springboard. Even though how the virus arrived in New York remains a mystery, the role the swollen mosquito population played in its spread is crystal clear. In the summer of 2000 the virus was back, identified in mosquitoes in New York's Central Park, and along with it came the helicopters.

Climate-related disease outbreaks in the US were

Increased range

Many highland regions in the tropic and temperate zones, previously too cold for mosquitoes, now provide hospitable temperatures for these disease-bearers. In the tropics, elevations at which temperatures are constantly freezing have climbed a full 500 feet in the past 30 years. Here's where the *Aedes aegypti* mosquitoes and mosquito-borne disease have emerged recently:

Malaria (spread by *Anopheles* mosquito)
Highlands of Ethiopia, Rwanda, Kenya,
Uganda and Zimbabwe,
Usambara Mountains, Tanzania
Highlands of Papua New Guinea and
West Papua (Irian Jaya)

Dengue fever
San Jose, Costa Rica
Taxco, Mexico

Aedes aegypti **mosquitoes**
(which spread both dengue and yellow fever)
Eastern Andes Mountains, Colombia, Northern highlands of India,
Highlands of Uganda, Ethiopia, Kenya and Rwanda

Scientific American, August 2000; The Heat Is On, Ross Gelbspan, Perseus Books, Massachusetts 1998.

nothing new – it is just that this particular story got reduced to a nifty heat sequence and many people made the link between the unusual weather and the outbreak.

Such outbreaks usually occur when a whole string of conditions is right (or wrong, as the case may be) and the weather pulls the trigger. Five years earlier a more baffling disease had grabbed the headlines. People in the US Southwest were coming down with a bug that advanced quickly from a flu-like fever to headaches, nausea and joint pains. But its primary symptom was difficulty in breathing, which progressed to a lethal inability to do so as fluid built up in the lungs. This was *hantavirus* pulmonary syndrome and its carrier was the humble deer mouse, a small rodent.

The virus exists either inactive or isolated in small rodent populations without much effect on humans, but when the conditions are right for a population explosion the story is quite different. In 1993 a prolonged spell of disturbed weather brought with it just those conditions. First a drought cut down the populations of the deer mice's enemies – birds of prey, coyotes and snakes. Then heavy rains early in the year brought plentiful grasshoppers and nuts for the mice to feed on. The mice wasted no time in breeding, setting off a sudden increase in the carriers of the virus. By summer drought conditions were back and the swollen ranks of deer mice left the open spaces to forage for food where humans lived. This close proximity brought what was then a mystery disease onto people's television screens.

In the same way that tiny particles of shed human skin can float around as motes of dust in our homes, particles of infected rodent urine, saliva and droppings got into the air in the form of a fine mist that was then inhaled. This was all it took to transmit this life-threatening disease. By autumn the deer mouse population had subsided and the outbreak came to an end. Later researchers would have to don head-to-foot protective clothing, looking a bit like astronauts, in order to study the disease in sealed deer mice pens. Today the US has early-warning systems in place and rodent populations are closely monitored, but the disease has emerged in Latin America, where such sophisticated methods of control may not be financially viable.

Borne on a buzz

Mosquitoes play the most significant role in projections of the climate-change induced spread of disease. They can relay malaria, dengue fever, yellow fever and many kinds of encephalitis. With growing drug-resistance and the decline in public health efforts in many developing countries, malaria today claims the lives of 3,000 people a day, the majority of them children. It is a disease that causes debilitating fever cycles that leave the sufferer feeling weak and sapped of strength. Its re-emergence in parts of Southern Europe and Russia, the Korean peninsula and the Indian Ocean coast of South Africa may be due to a range of environmental and human factors. But its emergence in highland areas can be more directly attributable to global warming. Some climate models foresee the zone of the disease encompassing 60 per cent of the world's people by the end of this century, adding an extra 50 to 80 million cases of malaria per year.[1]

The changing climate can influence the transmission of malaria in different ways. Prolonged warm periods above 60°F (16°C) are a precondition for *Anopheles* mosquitoes to transmit the most virulent malaria parasite *Plasmodium falciparum.* As it gets warmer, mosquitoes breed rapidly and bite more often. The parasite itself halves the time in which it develops fully in the mosquito's body during hot spells, doubling the chance that it will be transmitted before the mosquito dies. But other intense weather phenomena such as flooding and droughts can play a role too – with pools being left behind as floods recede and streams becoming stagnant during droughts.

Also broadening its range, piggybacking on *Aedes*

aegypti mosquitoes, is dengue fever which prefers temperatures that do not often fall below 50° F (10° C). No accurate treatment for it exists and its nickname – breakbone fever – gives some indication of the severe pain associated with it. People who have contracted dengue liken it to arthritic pain, but far worse – as if their bones would snap. In its hemorrhagic form dengue can be fatal. Up to 100 million people contract dengue fever each year and in the past decade its range has widened in the Americas and crept up to northern Australia.[2] Previously *Aedes aegypti* were confined to altitudes below 3,000 feet (1,000 meters), but now they have been found as high up as 6,600 feet (2,200 meters) in Colombia.[3]

Disease in a world divided

One of the ways of combating the spread of disease in a warming world would be to take intensified adaptive steps. This would mean improving surveillance systems and, once potential threats were spotted, taking measures to limit the populations of carriers of the disease, advising people on protective measures they could take and providing preventive medicine where possible. Many industrialized nations already do this, whilst many poorer countries, which find even basic health care provision a struggle, fail. If climate change increases the potential for outbreaks of disease, the fallout would once again be greater in the Majority World.

As it is, recent disasters have taken a heavy human toll. In February 2000 freak cyclones and heavy rains flooded large parts of southern Africa. The television cameras captured dramatic footage of bodies swept away, but did not stay to witness the aftermath – the spread of malaria and cholera in Mozambique and Madagascar. Two years earlier when Hurricane Mitch had hit Honduras in Central America, the devastation and loss of human life did not end with the homes swept away and the mudslides. An unholy trinity of cholera, malaria and dengue fever marched in to prolong the misery. In Kenya, unseasonably heavy rains in early 1998 caused a cattle disease called Rift Valley Fever to jump the species barrier and kill more than a thousand people within a few weeks. Such epidemics following natural disasters can stop development in its tracks for years.

As climate change throws up longer-lasting extreme weather and sudden dramatic changes, a rise in waterborne diseases can be expected, especially in regions with a weakened infrastructure. Dysentery and cholera often emerge in refugee camps following relatively short spells of rainfall because people are at their most vulnerable, living close to the elements with no access to a safe water supply or adequate sanitation. But severe weather can also threaten those who are not quite as vulnerable as refugees in camps. Droughts can drive people to unsafe water sources and increase the number of contaminants in the water available. Water scarcity also affects basic hygiene. In the case of floods, sewage and fertilizer can get swept into the drinking water supply, especially when livestock farms are situated close to water channels. These contaminants can cause algae blooms in the water making fish unsafe to eat and providing breeding grounds for cholera.

All of this is nothing new. It is just that a changing climate will tip the ecological balance that keeps many of these diseases at bay more often. The massive cholera epidemic of 1991 that spread from a port town in Peru to Ecuador, Colombia, Chile, Guatemala, Mexico, Panama and Brazil and which infected more than half a million and killed 5,000 is one such fearful example. Where it all began in Chimbote, Peru, unusual weather provided the ideal conditions. Along the coast there were widespread blooms of algae due to warm surface waters, making them a nutrient-rich soup. This was coupled with severe, unseasonal floods which tipped sewage into the water supply and started off the chain of infections.[3] The epidemic cost Peru $1 billion in lost tourist revenue and seafood exports.[4]

With this Pandora's box of sickness in mind, the health benefits of a warming world seem slight. Superhot temperatures in the tropics could reduce the *schistosomiasis*-bearing snail population. Milder winters in colder regions could reduce cold-related heart attacks and breathing problems, but the number of lives thus saved would not be much of an improvement on the numbers lost due to increased heat stress.[2]

Fumes and food

In this assessment of future ills that could result from climate change the focus has been mainly on the spread of infectious disease. But there is another more direct link with health and human meddling with the climate – one that is evident before climatic changes make their presence felt. A few years ago redevelopment along the M40 highway leading into London brought with it miles of temporary wooden walls and a resultant rash of graffiti. However this latter had nothing to do with the mindless attempts at profanity that are often the métier of fly-by-night daubers. Instead message after message bemoaned the ills of traffic congestion in the capital and the resultant high levels of asthma among children living along that particular stretch of highway. It must be remembered that the pollution that causes a build-up of greenhouse gases in the atmosphere often has much more direct effects on human health. Cities where skies are obscured by the emissions of industry and exhausts from thousands of stalled and wheezing cars have higher rates of asthma and cardio-respiratory disorders.

The changing climate will also have implications for food production (see chapter 4). The Hadley Center of the British Meteorological Office predicts that despite regional variations the negative changes in food production will be most marked in the tropics, with Africa being the worst affected. In Africa a predicted 18 per cent more people will be at risk of hunger due to climate change alone by 2050 and the forecast for tropical South America is also bleak. Needless to add these are regions which can ill afford to sustain such losses in food production, as already shortages are by no means remarkable events.

For subsistence farmers on marginal and vulnerable lands, relatively slight changes in rainfall could have

A plague on all your houses

Historian **David Keys**, author of Catastrophe: an Investigation into the Origins of the Modern World, gives his view of the plague epidemic that swept the 6th century – and his belief that its origins lay in climate chaos.

'With some people it began in the head, made the eyes bloody and the face swollen, descended to the throat and then removed them from Mankind. With others, there was a flowing of the bowels. Some came out in buboes [pus-filled swellings] which gave rise to great fevers, and they would die two or three days later with their minds in the same state as those who had suffered nothing and with their bodies still robust. Others lost their senses before dying. Malignant pustules erupted and did away with them. Sometimes people were afflicted once or twice and then recovered, only to fall victim a third time and then succumb.'

Thus wrote the 6th-century church historian Evagrius, describing the gruesome symptoms of the bubonic plague that devastated the Roman Empire and much of the wider world in the 6th and 7th centuries, the so-called Dark Ages.

By decimating populations and wrecking economies, the plague transformed the history of the eastern Mediterranean, Western Europe, the Middle East and Africa. In a sense, it was the final nail in the coffin of the Classical World and helped give birth to a string of modern European nations – England, Ireland, France and Spain. But the plague was not sim ply a disaster that erupted out of nowhere. My research over the past four years shows that it was almost certainly triggered by the climatic chaos of the mid-sixth century AD. It seems that the disease had long been endemic among wild rodent populations in East Africa - but it was the climatic disaster following 535 AD that enabled the disease to spread outside its normal territory.

The climatic situation (probably cooler, drier weather followed by floods) helped the plague bacillus in three key ways. Cooler weather increased the population of the fleas which carried the bacillus in their gut. It also forced the fleas to bite more rodents and other mammals because cooler temperatures prevented the bacillus releasing a natural anticoagulant in the flea's gut, a failure that resulted in the flea becoming ravenously hungry as its gut was blocked by blood clots. Third, the climatic chaos destabilized the relationship between predators and their rodent prey – a destabilization which led to a breeding explosion by the flea's rodent hosts.

intensely magnified effects, as food production is a challenge on such lands anyway. Cynics would argue that the real reason is that overpopulation drives people to farm on marginal land. However, population is only a part of the picture with dispossession due to poverty and resource-grabbing by the rich playing a much more significant role. The Hadley Center calculates that 'the

Once the disease had broken out of its normal territory, it appears to have spread throughout much of Africa – and northwards into the Mediterranean world. Its journey to Europe and the Middle East was by way of the Red Sea and the Roman equivalent of the Suez Canal – and was almost certainly transmitted courtesy of Roman greed for African elephant ivory. It was probably the ivory-trade vessels that introduced bubonic plague into the Mediterranean world.

I believe that in Africa it killed off the continent's major ancient ports. Indeed to this day their precise locations are a complete mystery to archaeologists. The plague also fundamentally changed the nature of the culture and the economy across vast swathes of eastern and southern Africa. Agriculture declined in many areas and pastoralism took over – almost certainly because plague-carrying rodents were more attracted to agricultural settlements and their stores of grain than they were to milk and meat on the hoof.

... and one recent instance of reemergence

In David Keys' account above, plague spread unchecked across the continents. It is the knowledge of the devastation wreaked by plague epidemics in the past that spread fear in Western India during the rainy season of 1994.

The outbreak began in the merchant city of Surat in Gujarat state. That summer temperatures had been sweltering and when the rains came they stayed longer than usual. The raised levels of humidity proved the trigger for a flea explosion in the city's grain-storage depots. As the rains continued, the drainage system became overwhelmed. As flood-waters rolled over the city streets, garbage bobbed up on them and spread out. Rats, surprised by the feast, lost no time in multiplying. After this it was the classic recipe of rats, fleas and eventual human infection, which then spread to hundreds of people. The news sent shockwaves through the country and beyond, making headlines in international news bulletins. Fears that people who had been infected might have traveled to the densely populated metropolis Mumbai (Bombay) sent the city's rat catchers onto red alert. There was talk of people not being allowed onto international flights from the area. Airline and hotel businesses lost over $42 billion as flights and hotel bookings got canceled. Meanwhile in Surat the municipal authorities swung into gear and had the streets lined with rat poison. Eventually the outbreak subsided, but not before it had shocked the world into realizing that plague had not gone away and that climatic extremes could wake it up. ∎

number of people at risk of hunger is projected to increase due to climate change by 30 million by the 2050s.'[5] This estimate does not account for large-scale catastrophic events or a spiraling cycle of positive feedbacks, so must be viewed as midrange. The threat of malnutrition and the increasing susceptibility to disease it brings is about as basic as you can get. Any food crisis is also a health crisis, as television images of famine remind us.

The health impacts of the deterioration of living conditions caused by rising sea levels, droughts and floods and other freak weather are determined not just by the phenomena themselves and the displacement they cause, but by a complex web of social and economic factors that sing along as a ghastly chorus to the health challenges. When the weather plays havoc with people's ability to work for their keep and harvest local resources, it compounds weakness and disease.

The ultimate health risk could be posed by a sudden flip in the global climate system caused by runaway feedbacks – making parts of the inhabited world much hotter or even much colder. The likelihood of this happening is fortunately still estimated as being relatively low, but there is no denying that it is distinctly probable. In such a scenario the health implications would not so much be about combating disease and hunger, though. Rather it would be a question of coping with the weather itself.

1 *World Disasters Report 1999*, International Federation of Red Cross and Red Crescent Societies, Geneva 1999. 2 'Is Global Warming Harmful to Health', Paul R Epstein, *Scientific American*, August 2000. 3 *The Heat is On*, Ross Gelbspan, Perseus Books, Massachusetts 1998. 4 'To save lives, give global warming the same priority as biological weapons, says WWF', World Wildlife Fund press release, 5 November, 1998. 5 'Climate change and its impacts', The Meteorological Office, London, November 1998.

4 Impacts: farming and food production

Farmers facing adversity... models for a warmer future and their limitations... the threat of rising seas... the problems besetting modern agriculture and how they would be amplified by climate change.

FARMERS ON THE whole are a canny lot, especially in regions where a single climatic phenomenon like seasonal rains determines their harvest. They are used to adapting what crops they grow judging by the kind of growing season expected. Indian food and trade policy analyst Devinder Sharma wrote about such adaptations to cope with the effects of the erratic monsoon of 1999 in many parts of India.[1] Discussing the situation in my home state of Madhya Pradesh in central India, he explained how the lateness of the monsoon had whittled away farmers' choices. In the first place they had to forego sowing their crops of choice – groundnuts and soybeans. But as August arrived with no sign of the monsoon, they had to abandon their usual standby of coarse millets. When the rains eventually turned up, a month after they were expected, the farmers had no choice but to plant low-yielding pulses making a last-ditch effort to put the available moisture to good use.

Sharma also wrote of the situation of farmer Chimanbhai Parmar from the neighboring state of Gujarat. The farmers in Parmar's village have been trying to get used to the fact that the monsoon, once a regular visitor in June, has in the last decade been behaving quite erratically. In 1999 with the arrival of the first showers more or less on time, Parmar and the farmers of his village praised the rain gods and set about planting groundnuts, their only cash crop. But the wait for the next set of showers, which usually follow in regular pulses, seemed to stretch out endlessly. 'Within a month of sowing, the plants had paled and withered in the scorching sun – fodder for the cattle to graze on.' Two months after sowing, his fields lay parched and barren. For miles around the same devastation was in evidence. Parmar, with three children to support, joined his fellow farmers in looking for non-agricultural work. Used as they were to hardship, their options were still unattractive to say the least – piecemeal work in local shops and factories or daily-wage labor for the Public Works Department, at less than a dollar a day.

In 2000 the monsoon was erratic once again. In Madhya Pradesh rainfall was far below the norm and had a knock-on impact on food prices and availability. What little rain they had was accompanied by baking temperatures, against which many young plants lost the fight. Temperatures above 104°F (40°C) can lead to wilting because they damage essential proteins in plants. With the heat-compacted soil turning warm, roots get affected, becoming less able to take up nutrients.

In the east of the country along the border with Bangladesh, torrential downpours brought floods

What farming contributes to the global greenhouse

Farmers release greenhouse gases in many ways. Carbon dioxide is released by clearing forests for crops, burning farm waste, and in the case of industrial agriculture, by use of fossil fuel energy to move heavy machinery and the production processes involved in the making of pesticides and fertilizers. Methane is released from rice paddies and large herds of cattle. Nitrogen oxide comes mainly from nitrogen-based fertilizers. The Intergovernmental Panel on Climate Change (IPCC) estimates that agriculture is responsible for 20 per cent of greenhouse gas emissions – via activities such as soil fertilization, cattle rearing and rice farming. A further 14 per cent is added by land-use changes, such as the clearing and burning of vegetation. Often such changes in land use are undertaken to clear land for farming. ■

'Potential Impacts of Climate Change on Agriculture and Food Supply,' Cynthia Rosenzweig and Daniel Hillel, 1995, www.gcrio.org/CONSEQUENCES/summer95/agriculture.html;
'Agriculture and Climate Change: a hard row to hoe,' Nick Sundt, July 2000, Global Change, www.globalchange.org/featall/2000winter2.htm

and the loss of over 1,200 lives. In Bangladesh three million were rendered homeless. When humans found it hard to survive the weather's onslaught, crops had little chance.

Meanwhile in Ethiopia, the rains failed for the fourth consecutive season and an international food aid effort bailed out the humans caught in the crisis, though many, especially children, died of hunger. For much of their cattle, fodder and water simply ran out. An elderly farmer, whose family had been forced to abandon their traditional pasture grounds for the safety of the nearest large village, bewilderedly told his BBC news interviewer that he hadn't witnessed such weather in 60 years of farming.

The outlook from climate models

Such tragedies put into sharper focus the shifts and changes in world agriculture predicted by the climate-modelers of the UK Meteorological Office's Hadley Center. Whilst the modelers talk in terms of general trends and percentages, the situation for the farmer on the ground can sometimes vary from one field to the next. The modelers, in their October 1999 impact assessment[2], worked out predictions on three emissions scenarios – 'business-as-usual' where there is no check on carbon dioxide emissions; an eventual stabilization of emissions at twice pre-industrial levels (550 parts per million – ppm) – in the atmosphere; and at thrice pre-industrial levels (750 ppm).

On the subject of water scarcity their conclusions are quite frankly frightening. Under a 'business-as-usual' scenario about three billion people will see an increase in 'water stress', with the biggest losers being northern Africa, the Middle East and the densely populated Indian subcontinent. The number goes down to one billion under the 550 ppm scenario, but shows little change from business-as-usual conditions under the 750 ppm one. This must be set against the shortages that are already in evidence in many parts of the world today and have become highly politicized issues. So far, so bad.

Those scientists involved in the predictions about food supply come up with three quite distinct conclusions for the three scenarios. The unifying thread is that the lower latitudes, in particular the arid and semi-arid regions of the tropics (where agriculture already poses great challenges), would witness drops in yields and increased risks of hunger. Increased carbon dioxide in the atmosphere could of course boost plant growth in some temperate regions especially for cereals such as wheat by speeding up the photosynthesis process by which plants make food. Such predictions have been eagerly seized upon by the fossil fuels lobby, which has promoted the idea of a future agricultural cornucopia

Very, very hungry

Despite the use annually of millions of tons of pesticides more than 40 per cent of the world's food crop is lost to pests, plant diseases and the effect of weeds – a yearly loss estimated at $500 billion.

Warmer temperatures and milder winters will offer improved opportunities to pests. They will be able to spread to higher latitudes and altitudes and benefit from a longer active period each year. Larvae may survive over winter in areas where they are killed off by the cold and cause major infestations when the next cropping season arrives. Insect pests are capable of producing numerous generations in a year with the females of some species producing hundreds of offspring. The kind of critical mass that locusts can generate – capable of stripping every field in their flight path – could become a reality for southern Europe. A rise in temperature of 1.8°F (1°C) would enable the European corn-borer to chomp its way 300 or so miles (500 kilometers) northwards. A 5.4°F (3°C) rise would see a profusion of insect pests, which would be difficult to control no matter how many chemical poisons one might fling at them.

Animal diseases such as African swine fever could migrate to North America. Plant diseases, especially of the fungal and bacterial variety, would luxuriate in warmer, wetter conditions. In Britain the milder winters are already prompting outbreaks of potato blight and mildew in cereals. ■

'A Hungrier World', Peter Bunyard, *The Ecologist*, March/April 1999;
'Potential Impacts of Climate Change on Agriculture and Food Supply',
Cynthia Rosenzweig and Daniel Hillel, 1995,
www.gcrio.org/CONSEQUENCES/summer95/agriculture.htmlx

with vigor.

But don't hold your breath. The scientists are not quite so enthusiastic: 'Many of these potential benefits are very small and are not significantly different from those arising due to natural decade-to-decade variability.' And there is the additional fact that not all food crops benefit from higher levels of carbon dioxide – corn/maize, sorghum, millet and sugarcane are some that lose out – whilst many aggressive weeds do. An increase in carbon dioxide would force plants to respire more rapidly. In hotter areas such as Southeast Asia and India a mere $0.9°F$ $(0.5°C)$ of further warming would lead to steep falls in rice and wheat production.[3] To say nothing of the explosion of crop pests that could occur (see box: Very, very hungry). Amongst the major losers in all scenarios are Africa, a continent where food production is already struggling to keep pace with population, and India – the world's second most populous nation – which so far has managed to feed its people. The US, the world's leading grain producer, could expect net gains under the 750 ppm scenario, but reductions under the 550 ppm one as wheat would benefit from increased levels of carbon dioxide in temperate latitudes.

The previous year's Hadley Center impact assessment had quoted a figure of 30 million additional people going hungry due to food shortfalls by the year 2050 and an additional 18 per cent of Africans facing the risk.[4] An earlier report by the Climate Institute had provided a starker outlook, estimating that 300 million people would face chronic malnutrition in sub-Saharan Africa alone by the year 2010.[3]

Startling as they might be, such global averages cannot hope to reproduce the necessary level of detail that would be required to give an accurate prediction for each region. The authors of the Hadley Center's 1999 report acknowledge as much: 'Note that this is a global and long-term assessment, focusing on average effects over space and time. At the local level (for example, in especially vulnerable areas) and over short periods (for example, in spells of drought or flooding) many of the effects of climate change on agriculture will be more adverse.' The devil, as they say, is in the detail.

With established patterns of weather being disrupted more frequently, it would matter little if the average annual rainfall or temperature evened out in the end, if within those averages lurked extremes that would damage the production of food. Also averages over relatively large geographical areas would be misleading if conditions in smaller food growing belts had been less than ideal. There is also the important consideration that all farming is dependent not just on rainfall but when that rainfall occurs – for example a prolonged hot and dry spell when the crop is coming into flower and the fruit forming can dramatically reduce yields.

The sea and salinity

Agriculture in proximity to densely populated coast-lines would suffer from rising sea levels. Seas will rise by half a meter by 2080 purely on account of the fact that warmer water takes up more volume. But if we add on the probability of significant melting of ice sheets in Greenland and the potential destabilization of the Western Antarctic Ice Sheet, the rise would be considerably higher. A 3-foot or 1-meter rise would put paid to a full third of the world's croplands. In low lying coastal areas where drainage is already a problem – amongst them parts of Egypt, Bangladesh, Indonesia, China, the Netherlands, Florida – it would be an uphill battle to sustain agriculture.[5] The sea's assault would be two-pronged, by creeping increases in salinity in soil and aquifers near the coast and by coastal flooding and storm surges. The experience of countries like Bangladesh in the recent past has been of surges raising a wall of water up to 18 feet (6 meters) high. One estimate suggests that in the next 50 years, surges in Bangladesh could cover up to 40 per cent of the country's land.[6] The scale of the environmental, refugee and food scarcity problems doesn't bear thinking about.

Tropical mangroves that protect against the infringement of sea water into croplands have been chopped down in order to raise shrimp destined mainly for consumers in the industrialized countries. In Thailand and in Bangladesh shrimp cultivation has led to the salinization of rice fields further inland. With the salt goes the crop and the land becomes barren. Sea water also penetrates where there is a gap created by the over-extraction of water from aquifers. In Egypt salinity has moved 22 miles (35 kilometers) up the Nile Delta[6] and the future for the country's farmers looks daunting with the prospect of coastal flooding and a drying up of the interior as a result of hotter temperatures.

In the constant search for greater productivity, irrigation has both answered prayers and given cause for new ones. Enabling farmers to grow up to three crops a year, irrigation accounts for 40 per cent of the world's food. But in the Majority World it also brings with it problems of salinity and saturation. So with old lands becoming unproductive, new fields must be found, usually at the expense of forests. Irrigation often relies on tapping water from deep underground aquifers, but many countries including the US have not been successful in drawing on this resource at a rate that would allow for replenishment. Grain and cotton farmers in the southern Great Plains continue to deplete the massive Ogallala aquifer.

It's a similar story in aquifers in California's Central Valley, home of half of the US's fruit and vegetable produce.[7] In the central states of India, the advent of tube wells seemed like the answer to the variability of the monsoon. Whereas traditional wells often ran dry during the wait for the monsoon rains, tube wells guaranteed a steady supply of water. Or they did until recently. Now water tables in many regions have dipped alarmingly and the tube wells are running dry. Efforts to sink them ever deeper bring little reward. Non-governmental organizations (NGOs) have embarked on massive educational programs, encouraging farmers to return to traditional water harvesting methods, which are based on saving water when it falls. Such methods, once widely employed and part of Indian farmers' environmentally-friendly ways of harnessing limited resources, had fallen into disuse, ironically enough, with the promise of piped water and tube wells.

Revolution gone sour

The challenges an increasingly populous world faces with respect to food production are already quite daunting – within a time frame of 30 years we are look-ing at doubling harvests, otherwise there could be shortages resulting in chaos. Whilst innovative schemes of sustainable agriculture are springing up in many of the poorer countries of the world particularly in Asia, as are communal efforts at growing and sharing food, the ravages of free market economics are also biting deep. For many farmers in the South, cash cropping is the only alternative to joining the ranks of the dispos-sessed in urban slums. There as elsewhere the Green Revolution – which got hijacked by richer farmers and transnationals that want a say in everything from what is grown to what fertilizers and pesticides are used and what price they are willing to pay for the end-product – has had less than green results. Originally intended as a short-term fix for farmers in countries with agricul-tural deficits, it birthed a kind of industrial farming that brings soil erosion, increased pesticide and fossil fuel use and water pollution in its wake

The problem of soil erosion is particularly acute, as one inch (2.5 cms) of topsoil takes around 500 years to form and is now being eroded at a rate that outstrips its replenishment. The loss in terms of nutrients has been estimated at close to the amount of fertilizer being used in the world's agriculture today. With higher temperatures heating up the soil, nutrient loss will speed up and the topsoil will get compacted and more prone to being washed away. We have seen already that the advance of desertification in marginal lands has been abetted by prolonged droughts (see box: A desert is born). When downpours follow on such droughts you can see the topsoil floating away in front of your eyes in the murky rush of floodwater.

Traditional methods of farming in India which emphasized subsistence crops over cash crops and which depended upon human and animal labor were derided in the heady early days of the Green Revolution. Instead a vision of modernity was pushed at an international level and promoted by an Indian

A desert is born

A leading expert with the UN World Meteorological Organization (WMO) believes that a systematic climate shift is afoot in Asia. Michael Coughlan who is director and coordinator of the climate activities programs at the WMO believes that the heavy floods in southern Asia and droughts across large Central Asian regions could suggest deeper climatic change rather than natural variation. He notes 'Our records only go back 100 years. But the rainfall and drought are in the extremes of what we have recorded over that time'.

On the eastern edge of the Qinghai-Tibet plateau a new desert is forming over what used to be rich pasture. As dunes erupt over clumps of tattered grass, the livelihoods of millions of herders and farmers who have nowhere else to go are at stake. Whilst the human factor of over-grazing has threatened the topsoil of the region, a decade of drier, warmer weather with three subsequent years of drought has pushed it over the edge. Tibetan herders from the region have been forced to become 'guerrilla grazers' according to the Chinese media, taking their animals to distant pastures already used by others.

Dr Song Yuqin of Beijing University reported the increase of barren areas in the semiarid lands stretching from Qinghai province through to Inner Mongolia and north of Beijing. In Mongolia a drought in 1999-2000 that left livestock devastated is assumed to be the main reason why the communists returned to power in the 2000 elections with an overwhelming majority. People were looking for desperate solutions in desperate times. ∎

'Asian floods, drought, sign of climate shift', James Poole, Reuters, 12 October, 2000; 'Chinese farmers see new desert erode their way of life', The New York Times, 30 July, 2000.

government aspiring to the success of the rich West. The cattle-drawn plow was replaced by the carbon dioxide spewing tractor, and dung used as fertilizer gave way to chemical fertilizers that released nitrous oxide into the atmosphere.

Such systems of farming necessarily benefited richer Indian farmers at the expense of the much more numerous poor. Indian environmentalist Vandana Shiva spelt out the implications way back in 1990: 'There is nothing inherently productive about agriculture based on oil and chemicals. In India traditional farmers use about half a calorie of clean renewable energy to produce one calorie of food, while highly mechanized, chemically-based agriculture uses ten calories of polluting, nonrenewable energy to produce one calorie of food.'[8] She had little time for lofty claims that this was 'helping' agriculture in countries like India: 'Aid for fertilizer, tractors, transport and energy mega-projects: all of these have primarily been ways for Western corporations to sell more machinery, equipment and engineering services to the Third World. For every dollar of aid given, three dollars' worth of business is generated in the industrialized countries.'

Shortages and inequity

On top of such ills that beset modern agriculture there is the naked fact of waste and want. In the US a government study revealed that more than a quarter of all food produced in the country doesn't get eaten,[9] while in the UK supermarket food capable of feeding 270,000 people ends up being trashed each year. With money-economies firmly in place, something as basic as food production is completely skewed by the demands of wealth. Industrial countries with about a quarter of the world's population, manage to use up about half of the world's grain, often feeding it to animals that will be eaten as meat.

Perhaps this would not matter so much if the rich countries were self-sufficient themselves – but they are not. They corner resources through the sheer power of money. This is where arguments about 'population control' in the developing South as a means of conserving resources and preventing environmental degradation seem to miss the point. If one starts from the premise upon which most declarations of rights are based, that every person is equal, then it should follow that each person has the same right to resources as everyone else. But if we look at the consumption of resources we see that the reality is vastly different. If population were measured in terms of the amount consumed, then the United States would have a population equivalent to twice that of China and nearly six times as large as India – the two most populous countries in the world.[10] Perhaps it would be wiser first to address such overconsumption, before 'overpopulation'.

Whilst many poor people in the Majority World work in conditions akin to slavery, producing crops for the world's food giants for a pittance and whilst speculators make their fortunes on the futures of these commodities, institutions like the World Bank insist on a 'level playing field' – that is, the removal of all

Water, wheat and beef

All farming needs water. But the amount of water needed to produce a pound of beef is far greater than that required for a pound of wheat.

 Amount of water required to produce 2.2 pounds of wheat: 2,113 pints (1 kg of wheat: 1,000 liters)

Amount of water required to produce 2.2 pounds of beef: 211,000 pints (1 kg of beef: 100,000 liters)

price supports which might bring these workers something more than a starvation wage.

If one then factors in extreme weather events and the possibility of more positive impacts in the richer North (and Australia) whilst the South suffers most of the fallout of the weather we are left not only with a vision as Argentinean diplomat Raul Estrada Oyuela put it of 'a green North and a brown South', but of a South where all forms of instability would be the order of the day. Climate change optimists take the line that the possible increased food production in the countries of the temperate latitudes could offset losses elsewhere – as if this excess food would just be given away to the disadvantaged. Environmental journalist Ross Gelbspan writes about the possible consequences of such a divide: 'The greenery of such a North would be deceptive. It would conceal a political and moral time bomb. It is hard to imagine that a society that fortresses itself against the rest of the world could continue to be an open society, vibrant with freedom, productively democratic, peaceful, and secure.'[3] Many Southern commentators would argue though that the economic stranglehold the North already has on their nations now calls into question any notions of an 'open society'.

Changes in the northern latitudes

But whether the outlook will really be quite so cozy for countries in the temperate latitudes is hotly contested and there are arguments aplenty why it may instead be deleterious. The US is currently responsible for nearly half the world's exports of grain. But in the past two decades droughts have been an increasingly frequent visitor in the US heartlands. The 1999 heat wave that killed over 270 people and thousands of fish also hit farmers hard. A $7.4 billion aid package was required to support them. After a record warm winter, government officials were looking at the prospect of drought yet again in 2000. In March the

US Agriculture Secretary said, 'We saw last summer just what a drought can do to farmers. Looking to the future, we need to be ahead of the curve, prepared for dry weather when it comes and equipped with the mechanisms that will protect farmers and prevent widespread losses.' Well the future arrived just a few months later, when heat waves and drought conditions returned and forests went up in smoke.

The long-term future looks likely to see further reprises of these conditions. Researchers of the National Oceanic and Atmospheric Administration (NOAA) predict that the central US will see 'substantial percentage reductions' in available moisture during the summer season by 2050 – more frequent drought conditions and reductions in yields of crops.[11] Many of the studies that talk of a more favorable outcome for US agriculture's adaptation to climate change assume the availability of water – with this essential assumption knocked out of the equation things begin to look very different indeed. Irrigation requirements would shoot up especially if warmer temperatures accompany the lack of rain and there are fears that the droughts could result in a return of the disastrous Dust Bowl conditions in the US Midwest.

What are the adaptive prospects available to the farmers of wealthy nations? Better management of resources and technological advances are mooted, as are the adoption of drought and pest resistant varieties of crops. The bottom line remains, however, that all such adaptations will require more capital outlay and crops that can grow in drier conditions will have lower yields. Northern Canada and Russia, similarly assumed to be beneficiaries of climate change, could also experience warmer drier summers. If, as models have predicted, the production of crops will become viable in the higher latitudes, several other issues are raised, such as the fact that conversion of land for farming purposes will release more carbon dioxide into the atmosphere when other vegetation is

removed. Soil fertility here is lower than in the traditional croplands and crops that are adapted to the
length of day in lower latitudes could react unpre-
dictably to longer daylight hours in the north,
possibly with early maturation that would reduce
yields. The outlook for Europe looks similarly dismal.
Areas *south* of 48 degrees north will get drier. In June
1999 Spain had the worst drought in 50 years wrecking agricultural production. Heat waves hit Greece
and surrounding countries in 2000. The rest is in for
soggier conditions. A recent study completed by
researchers Vellinga and Van Verseveld of the Free
University Amsterdam forecasts rainfall more akin to
tropical regions and frequent flooding to become a
'normal' feature of the weather for northwest Europe.
In September 2000, due to the increased instances of
localized flooding, the BBC weather team introduced
a new flood symbol for their television forecasts.
Vellinga and Van Verseveld's study, which examined a
wide range of international meteorological literature
and statistics from insurance companies, claims that
the connection between extreme rainfall and the
greenhouse effect is now indisputable.

What all of this means to farmers is becoming more
clear with each passing year. Australia's New South
Wales, for example, suffered three years of drought
followed by floods in November 2000 which have put
paid to agricultural production. Should the disastrous
scenario of the Gulf Stream stalling early in the next
century (see chapter 1) come to pass and leave northern Europe under snow for six months at a time,
current debates about agricultural adaptation would
become academic.

In Britain too the effects have been felt. One small
grower of organic vegetables noted: 'We have had
some very funny weather since last October; no frosts,
no real cold weather only rain and more rain. Seeds
and potatoes were late going in so with the rain they
went rotten in the ground. This is the first time we

have had to buy new potatoes in 16 years. Onions like golf balls in size, leeks that we could not get out of the ground, no marrows, no tomatoes. Beans seem to be going well, plenty of flowers, but no bees to pollinate them, so we shall have to wait and see.'

Whilst scientific models of the changing climate's impacts on agriculture attempt to grapple with the quantity and complexities of the factors involved, ordinary people who take pride in growing things have taken note what the weather is throwing at them and they're waiting to see what happens next.

1 'The fight for food', Devinder Sharma, *New Internationalist*, December 1999. 2 'Climate Change and its impacts: Stabilization of CO^2 in the atmosphere', The Hadley Center for Climate Prediction and Research, The Meteorological Office, October 1999. 3 *The Heat is On*, Ross Gelbspan, Perseus Books, Massachusetts 1998. 4 'Climate change and its impacts', The Hadley Center for Climate Prediction and Research, The Meteorological Office, November 1998. 5 'Potential Impacts of Climate Change on Agriculture and Food Supply', Cynthia Rosenzweig and Daniel Hillel, 1995, www.gcrio.org/CONSEQUENCES/summer95/agriculture.html 6 'A Hungrier World', Peter Bunyard, *The Ecologist*, March/April 1999. 7 'Troubled waters', Sandra Postel, *Utne Reader*, July/August 2000. 8 'Cry foul, cry freedom', Vandana Shiva, *New Internationalist*, April 1990. 9 *Colors*, October/November 2000. 10 'Consumption: Introduction', Kennedy Graham, in *The Planetary Interest* edited by Kennedy Graham, UCL Press, London 1999. 11 'Agriculture and Climate Change: A hard row to hoe', Nick Sundt, July 2000, Global Change, www.globalchange.org/featall/2000winter2.htm

5 Impacts: wildlife and forests

The first extinction caused by climate change... coral reefs in crisis... the threats to polar wildlife... would animals and plants be able to adapt?

IT'S DELICATE, TINY, more orange than golden, and presumed extinct. The golden toad of Costa Rica holds the dubious distinction of being the first extinction that can be laid at the door of climate change.

A former denizen of the misty, humid cloud forests near Monteverde in Costa Rica, its demise is being blamed on rising temperatures. The ecology of the cloud forests is dependent on such humid conditions. But with temperatures rising, the air has been getting less humid in the forests since the mid-1970s. Clouds in the Costa Rican mountains now form at much higher altitudes, so mists are also becoming less common. All this spelt disaster for the moist, lustrous, breathing skin of the golden toad. For many of the other frogs, toads and salamanders of the cloud forests, the changes are believed to have triggered disease outbreaks such as fungal infections that affect the skins of these amphibians. Researchers studying a 7,400-acre area (30 square kilometers) in the forest say that 20 out of 50 species of frogs and toads have disappeared. Forest lizards that are not susceptible to such fungal infections have also disappeared and climate change rather than a specific infection is viewed as a likely culprit.

But where there are losers there are also winners – in the cloud forests they happen to be birds. Fifteen bird species have moved in where they previously never ventured, including a species of toucan that formerly contented itself by breeding only in the lowlands and foothills rather than in the mountains proper.

It seems highly likely that there are other extinctions that have originated from climate change, but which have not been recorded. An escalating pace of change is putting additional stress on species that may be feeling the brunt of other environmental changes caused by humans, such as deforestation and water pollution. The case of the golden toad shows some of the susceptibilities that other species might also share. The toad had a limited habitat and was adapted to a set of very well-defined climatic conditions. It belonged to a family of creatures that are highly sensitive to rising temperatures and Ultraviolet radiation. Frogs and toads worldwide are showing freakish deformities and skin abnormalities (including albinism), with ozone depletion and chemical pollutants playing a role alongside climate change.

But climate change damages wildlife in other ways as well – by causing ripples in the food chain when certain species begin to lose ground, migrate or decline in numbers, by altering the physical environment, and by upsetting predator-prey balances, which usually result in explosions of the populations of animals that are pests to humans such as rodents and mosquitoes. Where animals are living in already fragile ecosystems, even slight changes can have far-reaching effects. But whereas some species' lives depend upon a fragile balance, others are hardier and can withstand a wider range of disturbances – cockroaches after all are said to have been with us since the time of the dinosaurs and will probably outlive human beings. Nevertheless climate change marching hand in hand with loss of habitat to human settlements and the numerous ecological blunders of humankind will put considerable stress on a wide range of wildlife – often to the detriment of human beings who depend on it.

Corals lose their colors

The world's coral reefs are a case in point. They lure legions of snorkeling and scuba-diving tourists each year. The vibrant displays of these gemlike creatures are the stuff of color supplements. But corals don't like heat, living in waters ranging from 64.4°F to 86°F (18°C to 30°C). With temperature changes of just 1.8°-3.6°F (1-2°C) above the maximum to which they are used, they become stressed and start to expel microscopic symbiotic algae known as *zooxanthellae*, thus ending a marriage which provides them with essential nutrients and their vivid colors. Their white limestone skeleton becomes exposed and death can result if the bleaching is sufficiently severe. In 1998, the hottest year on record since temperature records began, bleaching affected most of the tropical coral reef systems encompassing those in Australia, the Indian Ocean, the Florida Keys, the Caribbean, the Red Sea and the Bahamas – leaving thousands of square miles of graveyard coral.

Such mass events of bleaching have only been reported since 1979 and none of the indigenous communities that have subsisted alongside coral reefs for thousands of years have a name for the phenomenon in their languages, suggesting that it is fairly recent and not a part of some ill-understood natural cycle. So what apart from the lives of the corals and the appreciation of their beauty hangs in the balance here? For countries associated with coral reefs, the livelihoods of entire communities. Australia's Great Barrier Reef draws in $1.5 billion in tourist revenue, Florida's reefs $2.5 billion and Caribbean reefs $140 billion. They also form some of the most species diverse ecosystems in the world and are nurseries for fish – around 25 per cent of the fish catch in developing countries comes from coral reef fisheries, providing a vital source of protein. Seeing as fish stocks worldwide are already in crisis due to over fishing, any decline in habitat would have a considerable knock-on effect.[1]

The reefs also have a role to play in defending low-lying coastal lands from storm surges and it is indeed ironic that just when the world's weather is growing

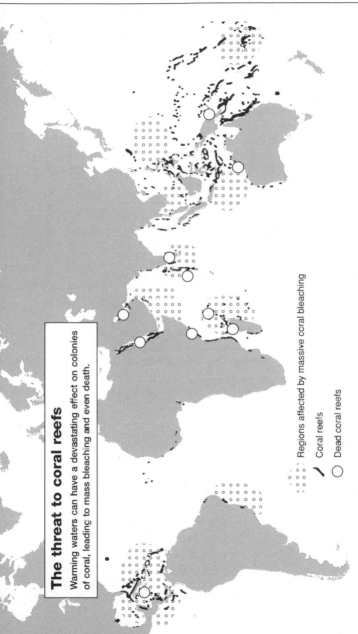

The threat to coral reefs

Warming waters can have a devastating effect on colonies of coral, leading to mass bleaching and even death.

Regions affected by massive coral bleaching

⌒ Coral reefs

◯ Dead coral reefs

increasingly stormier this line of defense is being weakened. Not all of the damage comes from warmer temperatures – reckless human activity features in the picture as well. Rainforest destruction increases sediment run-off that can smother and kill corals. In Sri Lanka parts of the coral reef that ringed the country's coastline have been destroyed for cement production purposes. In 1986, with the monsoon in full fury, storm surges tore up beaches, houses and railway lines along the coast. The damage was more pronounced where the reef had been broken up.[2]

Whereas coral reefs recover in time from bleaching incidents, in extreme circumstances these can result in coral death. But with ever-increasing episodes of bleaching, recovery may become increasingly difficult and the composition of the reefs could change utterly. While corals of the genus *Porites* are better able to resist higher temperatures and recover fully after bleaching, others of the genus *Acropora* are much more sensitive. Up to 95 per cent of them may bleach and subsequently die in the months that follow. They are clearly showing little sign of being able to adapt at a fast enough rate to rising temperatures. Eventually if coral reefs reduce in size they may have their very own contribution to make to climate change, for they are yet another sink for carbon dioxide, binding it to form limestone.

Fish feel the heat

Also feeling the heat are species of North Pacific salmon whose populations crashed in 1997 and 1998 as ocean temperatures hit abnormal highs – up to 10.8° Fahrenheit (6° Celsius) warmer than normal in one instance. Pacific salmon have already begun moving further north towards the Bering Sea to escape warming temperatures. In the North Sea, cod – the favorite of Britain's fish and chip establishments – are fast disappearing. Overfishing plays a major part in the North Sea cod's decline with fish often being caught before they are sexually mature and have had time to spawn, but the fish's sensitivity to rising temperatures is also indicated. A UK Ministry of Agriculture report established this link, saying the warmest temperatures in the 30 years the fish have been studied have resulted in dwindling stocks. Fishers who once netted the fish are trying to make a living from catching whelks and shrimps instead. The temperature link was demonstrated by the unusually cold spring of 1996 that caused the fish to spawn in great numbers, resulting in a bumper catch in 1998. What fishers in the region hope for more than ever is a repeat of such cold conditions, but the weather since has shown no signs of obliging.[3]

Movers and stayers

One of the most predictable impacts of climate change on wildlife has been shifts in the distribution of species, causing interlopers from what were previously warmer climes to move outwards, away from the tropics and upwards to higher elevations than before. A study that tracked 14 species of European butterflies has found that nine of them have ranged further north by more than 120 miles (200 kilometers) during the warmer years of the late 1990s.[4] Similar muscling in on other species' territory has been reported in

The changing of the seasons

- Spring now arrives three weeks earlier in the US.
- In Britain 20 bird species have been found to nest on average nine days earlier than they previously did.
- In southern England, the Marsham family has kept records of the 'indications of spring' since 1736. Thanks to their efforts it is known that the four earliest dates for oak trees to come into leaf all occurred in the 1990s.
- Tree and small animal species are migrating northwards in Canada in response to warmer temperatures.
- In the past 30 years, the arrival of autumn has been delayed in Britain by two days every decade. Spring's advance has been by six days every decade. ■

many marine organisms.

Apart from the phenomenon of new species moving into the happy hunting grounds of older residents and its resultant problems, there are additional difficulties raised by the shifting of temperature zones. Whilst one may marvel at reports of Alpine plants climbing ever higher to stay within the temperature bands they prefer (though this inevitably means that the area of habitat that is suitable to them will keep diminishing in size), there are other more unfortunate species of plants and animals that are finding it difficult to keep pace with the rate of climate change. Sometimes it is not the species concerned themselves but the other species that they depend upon for food or shelter that have not dispersed to more suitable areas. But the leanest times are for those animals that have nowhere else to go, having already reached the limits of their range.

On the other side of the world, this is the sad fate that seems to have befallen the Adélie penguin. Nesting in colonies on the shingle beaches of the Antarctic the birds are adapted to living in what for most other creatures would be a supremely hostile environment. But warmer temperatures are leading to more snow due to increased levels of water vapor in the air, which in the spring when eggs are laid takes longer to melt away. When the snow finally melts it can leave eggs lying in cold puddles of water or even drown newly hatched chicks. When this happens over consecutive years it can lead to entire colonies being deserted. Some move on to form another colony perhaps a bit further south, but there aren't many places that are suitable.

Another problem relates to a reduction in the amount of winter ice that forms on the waters where they feed. Under the ice, on the surface of the water sit algae, the first step in the Antarctic food chain. With less ice, there are fewer algae. Algae are eaten by krill that in turn form food for the penguins. So with amounts of krill also reduced the penguins begin to starve. The result has been decreasing populations in many colonies and the total disappearance of some.

When there isn't enough time to hunt

At the other end of the world a giant held in awe for its hunting prowess is being forced to go on a starvation diet. The Canadian Wildlife Service has been measuring the increasing skinniness of Arctic polar bears. Sedating the animals with tranquilizer darts, the researchers have been measuring body fat levels. The bears' major hunting season is in winter when they range across the Arctic sea-ice to gorge on seals and other marine animals, building up a layer of fat upon which they draw during the lean times when the ice has retreated. They are used to going without a feed for months at a time as long as they have hunted well during winter. But with the big freeze happening ever later in the season, the spring thaw returning earlier and the ice breaking up faster than usual, their hunting time on the sea-ice has been shortened. This shortfall of food is not just putting adult lives at risk – the next generation is particularly vulnerable. Increasingly researchers are finding that females are unable to successfully raise the pair of cubs they usually have in a

---

Water birds

The Arctic Tundra, a breeding ground for millions of water birds, could start giving way to northward moving forests as a result of warmer temperatures. More than half of all water bird populations could disappear as a result.

The World Wildlife Fund (WWF) estimates that a 40-57 per cent loss of tundra would mean that 4-5 million geese and about 7.5 million Calidrid waders would be without a habitat by the end of the century or earlier.

The worst affected will be birds which are already endangered – the Red Breasted Goose, the Tundra Bean Goose, the Spoon-Billed Sandpiper, the Emperor Goose and the Greenland White Fronted Goose. ■

'Climate change threatens rare Arctic Water Birds', World Wildlife Fund, 3 April, 2000, www.panda.org/climate/birds_pr.cfm

litter, during the years when they are reliant on their mother's hunting skills. By the middle of the lean season, it becomes evident that maybe one or both cubs may not make it through to the next hunting season.

The pack ice of the Arctic is home to several communities of animals from microscopic zooplankton to large blubbery walrus and often what isn't good for the polar bears isn't good for others as well. If sea ice shrinks it would spell disaster for the various kinds of seals and walrus. Walrus need to be in shallower waters to be able to dive to the bottom and feed. Upon their reemergence the ice needs to be thin enough for them to be able to break through but thick enough to support their 2,400-pound (1,000 kilograms) weight. Seals use the ice as a convenient fishing platform, also preferring to scour the depths of shallower waters for their food. In the Alaskan Arctic, ringed seals use land fast ice and stable pack ice for birthing. They dig lairs in the snow that has fallen on the ice in order to protect their pups that are born in late March and early April. The pups lie here for several weeks safe from the howling Arctic winter. But should the ice break up early or rain fall to collapse the snow walls of the lairs, the chances of the pups surviving take a plunge.[5]

Seabirds gather at the interface of ice and water in the Arctic, feeding on the plentiful supply of fish. In 1997 thousands of Alaskan seabirds died as a result of unusually warm surface waters. Their fish prey, stressed by the warmer temperatures, retreated down into deeper waters, beyond the point to which the birds could dive. The birds starved to death.[5]

This localized instance is symptomatic of thousands of others poised to occur or already occurring. Whilst the tendency of migratory birds to leave for cooler climes earlier and stay there longer has already been observed in many parts of the world, most notably by octogenarian Elizabeth Losey in Michigan who has been recording arrival and departure dates for more than 30 years, there are also reports of migratory birds getting confused by the changing weather patterns.

No place to call home

Loss of habitat is a very real threat as droughts could affect wetland dwellers and rising seas wipe out coastal colonies. Writing in *The Ecologist* magazine, Simon Retallack outlined the dangers: 'Sea-level rise, combined in some cases with developmental pressures [if climate change is not mitigated], will result in "about 40-50 per cent of the world's coastal wetlands being lost" by the 2080s, according to the Hadley Center – a staggering loss. Under threat are the vast tracts of tidal mudflats, salt marshes and sand dunes of the Netherlands, Germany and Denmark which are the feeding and recuperating grounds for many migrating

Shrinking habitats

35 per cent of the world's existing terrestrial habitats could be destroyed by the end of this century. There can be no guarantees that they would be replaced by the formation of new habitats of similar ecological diversity, especially when one takes into account human population pressure. Extinctions of both plant and animal species would be a certainty.

Rare species or those living in unique, isolated habitats would be the first to vanish. Possible future extinctions due to climate change could include Ethiopia's Gelada baboon, Australia's mountain pygmy possum, the monarch butterfly at its Mexican wintering grounds and the spoon-billed sandpiper at its breeding sites in Arctic Russia.

The loss of species could be as high as 20 per cent in the most vulnerable Arctic and mountainous habitats. The regions under greatest threat include parts of eastern Siberia, northern Alaska, Canadian boreal/taiga ecosystems, the southern Canadian Arctic islands, northern Scandinavia, western Greenland, eastern Argentina, Lesotho, the Tibetan plateau and southeast Australia.

The greatest loss of habitat would occur in the upper northern latitudes where the fastest rates of warming are being recorded. Up to 70 per cent of habitat could be lost in the higher latitudes of Canada, Russia and Scandinavia. Slated for a 45 per cent or greater loss are Russia, Canada, Kyrgystan, Norway, Sweden, Finland, Latvia, Uruguay, Bhutan and Mongolia. ∎

'Global Warming and Terrestrial Biodiversity Decline', World Wildlife Fund August 2000.

birds and which contain 50 per cent of the world's population of Brent Geese. Also threatened by rising sea-levels are the wetlands of the Mediterranean, the deltas of the Nile in Egypt, the Camargue in France, the Po in Italy, the Ebro in Spain which is lived in or visited by more than 300 species of birds, and over 13,000 hectares [30,000 acres] of English shoreline, much of it vital wildlife habitat, which according to English Nature will disappear in the next 20 years. Climate change is also predicted to lead to the disappearance of the mangrove forests of the west African coast, east Asia, Australia and Papua New Guinea, which act as breeding and feeding grounds for many fish and other marine and bird species.'[6]

What climate history tells us in relation to wildlife is that gradual change is answered by corresponding adaptation – grazing herds move along the line of the shifting vegetation taking the carnivores in pursuit. Catastrophic change alters the distribution of species completely as evidenced by the dinosaurs. Eventually when an ecological balance is struck again centuries later it is a radically different one from that which went before. The phase of change that humankind appears to have engineered at the moment is not catastrophic yet, but the danger is that it is far too rapid for adaptation to take place successfully both at a biological level as well as in terms of migration (see box: Shrinking habitats). A recent World Wildlife Fund (WWF) report suggests that the required migration rates for plant species due to climate change would be ten times greater than those recorded during the last ice age.[7]

Fenced in

In many parts of the world, species higher up in the food chain are corralled into enclaves and reserves, surrounded by humans, often competing for the same resources. A surreal incident in March 2000 where 8 monkeys died and 10 people were injured in drought-stricken northern Kenya after a two-hour clash over a tanker of water illustrates how the fundamentals of life are the same across species. Should the climate necessitate mass migration, many animal species would have nowhere to go. As the home turf for species gets smaller their diversity gets threatened, whilst invasive species that are capable of quick reproduction and wide dispersal – pests and weeds – would have a field day.

If shifting territories would be difficult for many animal species, it would be no easier for trees that rely on their seeds being carried by the wind, birds or rodents. Fossil records have been studied to reveal the speed at which plant species have migrated during changing climatic conditions in the past. They indicate that the slowcoaches of the plant world are capable of moving about 120 feet (0.04 kilometers) a year, whilst the swiftest specimens can achieve speeds of 1.2 miles or 2

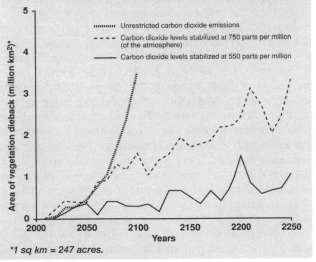

Vegetation dieback

When the area that was previously under vegetation has less than 10 per cent of its vegetative cover remaining it is said to be suffering vegetation dieback. The graph below shows the predicted increase in vegetation dieback as a result of increases in carbon dioxide concentrations.

*1 sq km = 247 acres.

The Hadley Center for Climate Prediction and Research, UK Meteorological Office.

kilometers a year. However, just taking into account changes in temperature alone, plant species in many parts of the world would need to be able to migrate at annual rates of between 0.9-3.4 miles (1.5-5.5 kilometers). Many would not be able to stay in the race.

Smoke signals from the world's forests

It's not as if the world's forests have it easy at present. Nearly half of the original forest cover of the world is gone and trees in many regions are weakened by air pollution. Whilst increased amounts of carbon dioxide in the air might give a boost to photosynthesis, it would also mean that trees would need better nutrients from the soil. If warmer air temperatures are added into the mix, then more moisture would be required, too. In regions with poor soils and low rainfall there could be major diebacks and loss of diversity rather than growth spurts. Warmer conditions would also favor diseases and pests. In Alaska, some 50 million acres (20 million hectares) of forest have been colonized by spruce bark beetles in an unprecedented attack, the fruit of several warm years in succession. Since 1989, 25 million trees have died as a result.[8]

Amongst forests identified as being particularly at risk by the WWF are the boreal and taiga forests stretching through the Arctic and sub-Arctic regions of Siberia, Scandinavia, Canada and Alaska. These forests are at the limits of their range and changing temperatures would mean a slow decline with grasslands, farming and northern deciduous forests chewing into their southern edges. Animal species like the woodland caribou, the wolverine and wood buffalo would get squeezed into a shrinking habitat. The northern boreal forests have swampy soils which are a primeval reservoir of vegetation that has lain in the ground for centuries, a gigantic store of carbon that could begin to leak were the forests to be disturbed and the soils to start drying out.

Tropical forests that already come in for the chop and see the fastest rate of extinctions of species could also suffer from a combination of intense heat and lack of rainfall. They would be particularly susceptible to fire. Take the tinder-dry forests of Indonesia where fires have been breaking out every summer since 1997. Between mid-1997 and early 1998 ten million hectares of pristine rainforest went up in smoke. These fires didn't begin with dry lightning strikes: they were started by people clearing land for farming. But the fact that the fires spun out of control can only be blamed on the unusually dry conditions. Endangered species like orang utans had to be rescued from the fires, though many perished. The fires created a billowing expanse of smog that caused ship collisions, traffic accidents and even an airplane crash. Neighboring

Tree trauma

The Earth's forests absorb CO_2, produce oxygen, anchor soils, moderate the climate, influence the water cycle and provide a rich habitat for myriad plants and animals.

- Half the world's original forest cover of some 7.5 billion acres (3 billion hectares) has been destroyed in the last 40 years; only 20% of what remains is undisturbed by human activities.
- More than 90% of forest loss is in the tropics; about 34.5 million acres (14 million hectares) of tropical forest are hacked down each year, two-thirds of that due to farmers clearing land.
- More than 90% of forests in the Mediterranean have been cut while from 1995 to 1997 more than 14.8m acres (60,000 sq kms) of forest cover in Brazil was destroyed – an area twice the size of Belgium. ■

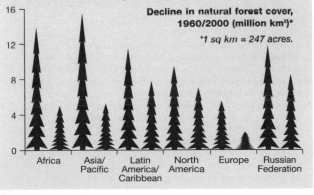

Decline in natural forest cover, 1960/2000 (million km²)*

*1 sq km = 247 acres.

Africa | Asia/Pacific | Latin America/Caribbean | North America | Europe | Russian Federation

Living Planet Report 1999, WWF International

Malaysia lost billions of dollars with tourists canceling holidays and airports closing.[9] This single conflagration's contribution to carbon dioxide emissions was equal to all the fossil fuels burned in Europe in a year.[8] In May 1999 forest fires blazed in the most unlikely of places due to dry and warm conditions – Siberia.

Also at risk are coastal mangroves that offer protection from storm surges to countries like Indonesia, Brazil and Bangladesh. Lying in the pathways to the sea, drawing their sustenance from submerged soils, they are fighting against rising sea levels which threaten to wash away the buildup of sediments these trees rely on. Similarly at the edge of their limits are high mountain forests that skirt the tree line – as tree species from the lower reaches of the mountains move upwards these forests would undergo a complete change in character.

In the summer of 2000 came reports that Alaska's white spruces, the most widespread species in North America, were sending out a distress signal, by leaking carbon dioxide into the air. The trees had stopped growing so fast as a result of climatic changes that they were actually releasing carbon instead of absorbing or 'sinking' it.

The world's forests are responsible for sinking a full quarter of humankind's emissions of carbon dioxide, acting, as the Hadley Center puts it, as a 'brake' on the rate of carbon dioxide increase and global warming. When forests suffer, the brakes fail.

1 *Climate change, coral bleaching and the future of the world's coral reefs*, Ove Hoegh-Guldberg, Greenpeace International, Amsterdam 1999. **2** *The Breakdown of Climate*, Peter Bunyard, Floris Books, Edinburgh 1999. **3** 'Cod disappearing from North Sea as it warms', Ian Herbert, *The Independent*, 12 May, 2000. **4** 'Edging towards meltdown', Julian Pettifer, *BBC Wildlife*, March 2000. **5** *Answers From the Ice Edge: the consequences of climate change on life in the Bering and Chukchi seas*, Margie Ann Gibson and Sallie B Schullinger, Greenpeace/Arctic Network, June 1998. **6** 'Wildlife in danger', Simon Retallack, *The Ecologist*, March/April 1999. **7** 'Global Warming and Terrestrial Biodiversity Decline', WWF, August 2000. **8** 'Nature's bottom line: climate protection and the carbon logic', Greenpeace, May 1999. **9** 'Breathtaking', Nicola Baird, *New Internationalist*, December 1999.

6 The politics of climate change

The origins of the climate debate... political double-speak and skeptics sponsored by fossil fuel industries attempt to sabotage negotiations... the Intergovernmental Panel on Climate Change issues assessments... US politics provides no answers... the convoluted road to emissions reductions and the loopholes in current agreements.

THERE IS A common human reaction to the possibility of terminal disease – 'It couldn't happen to me'. It exists even when there is a rational understanding of the degree of risk and one has known other people who have suffered. Sometimes it persists even after diagnosis. Denial is a common enough reaction to unpleasant truths.

Denial also features heavily in reactions to the projected catastrophes of climate change. Many people still think we have got time to make up our minds about what we are going to do about the problem. Perhaps it's inertia, perhaps fear of the radical changes that would be necessary. Even though rationally the message may have got through that action on emissions reduction cannot wait and the issue is a burning one, we are often content to let it smolder. In fairness the enormity of the problem can be baffling, but there remains a niggling feeling that if enough people would actively voice their concern they would possibly achieve more than that achieved by over a decade of political wrangling.

Ostrich arena

For it is in the political arena – where the ostrich tendency of sticking one's head in the sand to avoid doing anything seems to predominate – that the battle for the world's weather is being fought. Typical of political skirmishes, this one is dirty, shortsighted in the extreme and miles from any real breakthrough.

Scientific concern over the possible greenhouse effect of certain gases in our environment has been around since the 1970s, with scientific speculation turning slowly into scientific consensus as actual increases in carbon dioxide concentrations began to be measured. In 1979 the World Meteorological Organization brought scientists together for the First World Climate Conference in Geneva, Switzerland, which issued a call to governments to 'prevent and prepare for the negative impacts of human induced climate change'. Six years later another conference in Villach, Austria, led to the inclusion of all greenhouse gases in assessments of global warming. When this was done the doubling of carbon dioxide equivalents was estimated as early as 2030. Calls for international cooperation to head off a climate crisis gained increased urgency.

But the issue began to be seriously addressed after a declaration in Washington that caught the attention of the world's most powerful nation. On 23 June 1988 James Hansen, a climate scientist with NASA's Goddard Institute, warned a Washington meeting that the world was getting warmer due to the build-up of greenhouse gases, and an increased tendency for droughts and floods was to be expected. He made his speech on the hottest day of that year in the US, at a time when the Midwest was in one of its worst droughts. It caught the attention of the sweltering policy-makers and population at large. Hansen's speech was a spur to the setting up by the United Nations of the Intergovernmental Panel on Climate Change (IPCC), a body with input from over 2,000 scientists from around the world. In their First Assessment Report in 1990 they stated that while they were unable to say that they had found the human impact on the climate as yet, it was clear that the increase of greenhouse gases would have an impact. By the time of their Second Assessment Report they would confirm 'a discernible human effect on global climate'. But right from the beginning the polit-ical battle lines were drawn, with the trillion-dollar-a-year oil and coal industries[1], the indus-trialized nations who were the big energy consumers and the fossil fuel producing countries realizing the threat any change in the status quo might bring. There was also another kind of politics underpinning why Hansen's speech had been taken seriously.

As Vandana Shiva, writing less than two years after the event, so acerbically put it: 'Thermometers regis-tering a few degrees more in the United States suddenly turned climate change into a 'global' issue. The entire scientific community was immediately mobilized.

'Contrast this with three years earlier when thou-sands of famine victims in Ethiopia and Sudan weren't enough to move governments in the North to respond to desertification and drought as global environmen-tal emergencies. True, they sent food aid, but the climate problem remained a local difficulty. These deaths, after all, took place in Africa – they were still "out there".'[2]

Shiva had put her finger on a bias that persists to date – the most-detailed impact assessments are still available for industrialized countries, despite the knowledge that poorer nations in tropical and semi-tropical regions will suffer more adverse impacts. The input of these nations in the climate debate is also much more likely to be talked down.

Back in 1988 Australia decided to host a national conference on the greenhouse effect whose delibera-tions were closely followed by an unexpectedly large number of people. But with each passing year devel-opments in climate change knowledge came under attack from industry-sponsored skeptics and self-interested politicians, raising a cloud of doubt over every new finding through propaganda and scare-mongering. Over the years as scientific consensus has overwhelmingly come to support the reality of climate

change these voices have shouted ever louder to por-
tray the issue as something scientists cannot agree
upon and about which there is reasonable doubt.

Since the late 1970s climatologists have been
attempting to work out the prospects for global warming and politicians had picked up on the issue –
former Soviet leader Mikhail Gorbachev, as leader of a
country whose heavy industry was notoriously energy
inefficient, often spoke of the perils of a warming
world. Even Britain's then Prime Minister, the right-
wing Margaret Thatcher – who had welcomed the
Falklands/Malvinas War in May 1982 by saying 'It's
exciting to have a real crisis on your hands, when you
have spent half your political life dealing with hum-
drum things like the environment' – was, as the
decade drew to a close, commenting increasingly on
the threat to a common future posed by climate
change. In November 1989 she said, with a remarkable
flash of prescience, that 'No issue will be more con-
tentious than the need to control emissions of carbon
dioxide... We can't just do nothing... Each country has
to contribute, and those countries who are industrialized must contribute more than those who are not.'

But Thatcher's government was not about to match
her words with deeds. That same month at a global
warming conference in the Netherlands, Britain was a
key opponent of a Dutch proposal to stabilize and
reduce carbon dioxide emissions. This was despite a
stated commitment by nations (albeit not legally binding) at a conference in Toronto the previous year to
reduce their greenhouse gas emissions. Such duplicity
was to become increasingly evident in the 1990s, with
political leaders making the right kinds of reassuring
noises that they were taking climate change seriously –
whilst their actions did little to support real change.

Battle commences

In May 1990 a hundred scientists of the IPCC gathered
in a country hotel in the UK to sort out the wording of

the final draft of their first Scientific Assessment Report. If they had hoped for seclusion, it was not to be – a media circus surrounded the hotel. Amongst the observers allowed to sit in on the deliberations were 11 scientists on the payroll of the fossil fuel industries. But they weren't quite observers in the traditional sense as they were allowed to make suggestions regarding the wording of the document.

Central to this first report was the link between carbon dioxide emissions and increases in the planet's temperature in the future. The IPCC at the time warned that the Earth could warm by as much as 8.1° F (4.5° C) with a doubling of carbon dioxide levels by around 2050. They would later reduce the upper estimate by 1.8° F (1° C) ironically enough due to the masking effect of projected increases of pollutants in the atmosphere. The message was clear. In order to stabilize atmospheric concentrations of carbon dioxide, a 50-70 per cent cut in emissions from human activities was required. To meet such a target an energy revolution would have to come about, one that would effectively sever humankind's dependence on fossil fuel energy.

As the summary of the report (which was destined for wide media attention) was being worked on, Dr Brian Flannery, a scientist on the payroll of Exxon, decided to intervene. The group he represented was called the International Petroleum Industries' Environmental Conservation Association, an image-conscious moniker that bears parallels with other such industry alliances and skeptical groups. Even bodies that dismiss the idea of climate change outright as nonsense are savvy enough to hide under the mask of environmental concern. Flannery suggested there were uncertainties about how carbon behaved in the climate system. The response from the IPCC scientists was that such uncertainties should not affect the ultimate goal of stabilizing the amount of carbon dioxide in the atmosphere, which could only be realized by radical cuts in emissions. Now Flannery changed tack and questioned the validity of the climate models the IPCC had used, calling their range 'scientifically uncertain'. Again the IPCC scientists begged to differ. Flannery's intervention was relatively mild compared to what the climate change skeptics would throw up in years to come but it was perfectly in character.

The day after Flannery's intervention Margaret Thatcher held a press conference at which she called the report 'an authoritative early-warning system.' Warming to the theme she spoke of some of the consequences: 'There would surely be a great migration of population away from the areas of the world liable to flooding, and from areas of declining rainfall and therefore of spreading desert. Those people will be crying out not for oil wells but for water.'[3]

To the fossil fuel industries, action on the emissions reductions front would come as a body-blow and they began organizing their armies of skeptics, PR spin-merchants and sympathetic politicians (these latter often represented constituencies where a large proportion of the workforce was involved in the fossil fuel industry and/or had received generous donations from the oil and coal giants). At stake were vast empires funded by the unhindered profits of a century of oil burning. The oil companies had already tracked down reserves holding more than the amount humans had consumed throughout history – and no doubt there were still reserves to detect. The coal industry was sitting on even larger reserves. Neither was about to let its lifeblood lie in the ground.

From now on both scientific discussion and political negotiations were open targets and when important meetings were held, along with the scientists, environmental non-governmental organizations (NGOs) and politicians would come members of what has been dubbed the 'Carbon Club'. They were invariably fronted by a handful of skeptical scientists acting as mouthpieces for seemingly innocuous sounding groups such as the Global Climate Coalition and the Global Climate Council. The Global Climate Coalition's list of membership and donors reads like a who's who of the major fossil fuel producers and consumers. The Global Climate Council was decidedly more secretive about its funding, but not in the least bit less vocal for all that.

The conspicuous persuaders

Such industry-funded scientists now took center-stage in any climate debate, turning in storming media performances. Against the vast array of IPCC scientists from all over the world, this motley group consisted of only a small number of very vocal nay-sayers, most of whom were not Cassandra-like prophets of doom crying in the wilderness but scientists whose research was not peer-reviewed or, allegedly, had been discredited. Some had not conducted any original research in years. It was a case of whoever pays the piper calls the tune and this group piped loud and clear for the world's media to hear. With just five industry-friendly media companies dominating the world's news channels, the skeptics were set for a long ride.

They used several factors to their advantage. Most news desks aim to maintain some kind of objectivity by giving space to opposing sides of an argument. In this case one of the 2,000-plus pro-climate change scientists would get the same amount of airtime as a representative from the handful of skeptics or an industry spokesperson. The skeptics were adept at getting the message across that there was little scientific consensus on the issue, when in fact the world's leading climatologists overwhelmingly agreed on the reality of climate change.

Industry also pulled no punches, confidently asserting that there was no danger, that any weather extremes that happened were just an expression of natural variability and had nothing to do with climate change and that if climate change did come about it would be actually beneficial. Spurious arguments would often be unnecessarily highlighted – such as the fact that as carbon dioxide levels rise in the atmosphere their ability to trap heat progressively declines. But such knowledge was already being taken into account in the IPCC's calculations. In the US the skeptics even argued that research shouldn't be funded by government departments, but should be left in the hands of the companies most affected by it, which is a bit like hiring a wolf to take care of sheep.

The confidence of the skeptics who made very definite pronouncements was in marked contrast to the rest of the scientific community who talk in terms of probabilities and possible outcomes and percentages.

Packaging Mitch

In the aftermath of Hurricane Mitch came a wave of denial about its possible origins. **Sheldon Rampton** *and* **John Stauber** *recount one skeptical voice's determination to shout louder than the rest.*

It was only natural to wonder if global warming was to blame for the disaster. 'This was perhaps what is becoming a typical disaster in today's world of El Niño and global change,' observed J Brian Atwood, head of the US Agency for International Development, which coordinated relief activities. Speaking to CBS News, he called the hurricane 'a classic greenhouse effect'.

For Patrick J Michaels, people like Atwood are part of the problem. Michaels, a professor of environmental science at the University of Virginia, penned an article titled 'Mitch – That Son of a Gun'. He attacked Atwood's remarks as 'White House huckstering... If there's any possible way to conflate human suffering with global warming, the Clinton administration will do so... Rumors persist that Vice President Gore has been advised to make global warming a central theme of his presidential run in 2000. Threatening hundreds of thousands with imminent drowning unless they vote for him is a crude but probably effective trick.'

Michaels' commentary was printed in the *Washington Times* and the *Journal of Commerce*. Rewritten as local editorials, it appeared in newspapers as far apart as the *Wisconsin State Journal* and the *Wyoming Tribune-Eagle*. 'Just how stupid does the Clinton administration think we are?' asked the version that appeared in the *Tribune-Eagle*.

Thus in the general perception scientists appeared to be uncertain on the issue when in reality they weren't and, worse, the skeptics sounded more convincing.

As if this wasn't bad enough, the political response to the IPCC's findings in no way reflected the urgency demanded by the science. In August 1990 after the fuss created by their first scientific assessment, the IPCC met again with government representatives in Sweden. Jeremy Leggett's account of this meeting in his book *The Carbon War* is revealing: '... the political geography was already clear. The IPCC's scientific working group had professed itself "certain" that global warming lay ahead unless greenhouse-gas emissions were cut. The impacts working group had predicted a collage of expanding environmental catastrophe should the IPCC scientists' predictions turn out to be

Stupid enough, apparently, that none of these outlets bothered to check Michaels' credentials. If they had, they would have found that Michaels is part of a small but vocal minority of industry-funded climatologists who dispute the mounting evidence that suggests that global warming is a consequence of modern industrial activities, such as the burning of fossil fuels. By his own account, Michaels has received more than $165,000 in funding from fuel companies, including funding for a non-peer-reviewed journal he edits called *World Climate Change*. He has served as a paid expert witness for utilities in lawsuits, appears on television and radio and testifies before government bodies. At the time Hurricane Mitch struck, he was also a 'senior fellow' at the Cato Institute, a right-wing, industry-funded think-tank that campaigns against 'unnecessary' and 'harmful' environmental regulations.

The use of scientists as spokespersons for corporate interests is an example of a public-relations strategy known within the trade as 'the third party technique'. Merrill Rose, executive vice-president of the public-relations firm Porter/Novelli, sums it up succinctly: 'Put your words in someone else's mouth.' Remember the TV commercials with actors in lab coats pretending to be doctors and claiming that nine out of ten of their colleagues prefer a specific brand of aspirin? With commercials you are on your guard. But put the message in the mouth of someone like Patrick Michaels and you have a 'real scientist' speaking. The commercial interests behind the message are much better disguised. ∎

From 'The junkyard dogs of science', *New Internationalist*, July 1999.

correct. But all that the policy responses working group had come up with, after 18 months of deliberation, was a toothless list of potential technologies which could help, in principle, with the limitation of greenhouse gases. This third working group was chaired by the United States.'[3]

Here it is pertinent to consider one fact: the US with 4 per cent of world population accounts for 36.1 per cent of the world's carbon dioxide emissions. When all greenhouse gases are taken into account the US contribution is nearly a quarter of the world's total. It follows that the deepest emissions cuts would have to be made by the US, a task most of its politicians have been loath to contemplate.

False parameters

After a series of governmental meetings, the stage was set for the UN's 1992 Rio de Janeiro Conference on Environment and Development (UNCED) at which more than 160 countries signed the Framework Convention on Climate Change before the largest media circus ever gathered in the world, numbering over 10,000 press representatives. The Framework Convention, designed to set industrialized countries down the path of emissions reductions, may have been a setback for the Carbon Club, but it was one from which they devised a strategy that was to have far-reaching repercussions. They now started pointing out the potential for future emissions increases by developing countries, thus attempting to deflect attention from the largest polluters.[3] The trick was to arouse enough indignation on the issue so that any discussions about emissions cuts by the industrialized nations would have to be linked to parallel cuts in countries like India and China whose emissions potential is great. This idea, which has stuck like a thorn in the side of subsequent climate change negotiations, is dismissed as nonsense by industrializing nations who argue that their historical contribution to greenhouse warming is minuscule. It is estimated that up to 90 per cent of greenhouse gases in the atmosphere arising out of human agency were emitted by the 20 per cent of people who live in industrialized countries. Having fossil fuel energy to thank for their global supremacy today, it is hypocrisy of the highest order to suggest that industrializing countries are on a level playing field and must compromise their future development in order to cushion the excesses of the rich West. Whilst there are many politicians in developing countries who argue that their countries should have the right to develop using fossil fuels, this is not to say that developing nations are against clean energy – they just want it at a price they can afford.

Towards the end of 1995 the IPCC completed its Second Assessment Report which found that 'a pattern of climatic response to human activities is identifiable in the climatological record'. It was the result of input from some 2000 scientists and followed findings by two major studies earlier that year that put paid to the argument that natural climatic variability was to thank for the heated 1980s and 1990s.

Republicans on the loose

However, none of this would faze Republican politicians in the US who, wooed by the oil and coal lobby, have consistently taken up cudgels to defend both industry's and the ordinary American's right to pollute. In the summer of 1995 Republican member of congress Robert Walker was the leading light in arguing for cuts in funding for a NASA program that aimed to monitor climate changes around the world. He succeeded in his mission, relying heavily on the findings of the Washington-based George C Marshall Institute that had confidently asserted that 'comparable temperature changes are commonplace in recent climate history'. According to environmental journalist Ross Gelbspan this is an organization 'which conducts no original research itself and whose reports are viewed by the vast majority of scientists as political statements rather than as research contributions.'[1]

Republican Dana Rohrabacher went one better when he presided over a series of House Science Subcommittee on Energy and the Environment hearings. Upon listening to an Environmental Protection Agency official talk of the potential rise in sea level over the next century being capable of drowning up to 60 per cent of the US's coastal wetlands, Rohrabacher's sage reply was, 'I am tempted to ask what this will do to the shape of the waves and rideability [sic] of the surf. But I will not do that. I will wait until later, when we get off record.'

In a hearing whose title – 'Scientific Integrity and the Public Trust' – was no doubt not intended to be ironic, Rohrabacher threw further pearls to his audience. Speaking about the ozone scare, he said it 'turned out to be another basically the sky-is-falling from an environmental Chicken Little, a cry we've heard before when the American people were scared into the immediate removal of asbestos from their schools.' That someone chairing a meeting on scientific issues should dispute the dangers of asbestos is beyond belief. At one point in the proceedings Rohrabacher found himself unable to remember the word 'hydrocarbons' and started speaking of carbohydrates instead. He also displayed a knack for the grandiloquent statement saying, 'The American people deserve better of their government than scare tactics that are designed to intimidate and repress rational discussion.'

The following year (1996), despite the publication of the IPCC's authoritative Second Assessment Report he told a budget meeting of the Science Committee, 'I think that money that goes into global warming research is really money right down a rat hole.' Rohrabacher is the most dangerous kind of climate change skeptic, not just one who refuses to engage with the science and persist in his own opinions, but one who wields political clout. In 1995 he had not only voted for exports of oil from Alaska's North Slope, an area of environmental fragility, but also blocked money that would have gone towards promoting the export of American solar technology.[1]

A way with words

The most quoted line from the IPCC's Second Assessment Report was 'the balance of evidence suggests there is a discernible human influence on global climate'. The elegance of its phrasing belies the heated discussions that went into key words. It had started life simply as, 'the changes point towards a human influence on climate.' But this was much too direct for the interested parties and 'the changes' got converted into 'the balance of evidence' with its implicit suggestion that there was significant evidence that pointed in the other direction as well.

Again 'a human influence' was too direct and one of the scientists suggested 'an appreciable human influence' before 'discernible' became the adjective to find favor. Delegates representing the Saudi Arabian and Kuwaiti governments, and briefed by prominent skeptic Washington attorney Don Pearlman (who represented coal and oil producers though he prefers not to say which), objected frequently. At one point Mohamed Al-Sabban, an oil ministry official from Saudi Arabia and veteran of climate negotiations suggested that 'Preliminary evidence which is subject to large uncertainty points towards a human influence.' The IPCC scientists, used to proceeding by scientific consensus found such negotiation over almost every line of their text both novel and wearing. So wearing in fact that by the time it came to be published the executive summary, the part that would be most widely consulted by the world's media had shrunk to a quarter of its original size mainly due to the constant stalling by vested interests.[3]

Between the discussions of the Report text and its appearance in print six months later in June 1996 the skeptics went into overdrive in their attempts to discredit the IPCC's findings. The Marshall Institute and Patrick Michaels both released reports aimed at kicking up a dust storm. The first asserted that there was 'no evidence' of human influence on climate change, whilst the second queried the use of ground-based temperature records in demonstrations of warming trends, claiming temperatures from the satellite record which measure temperatures throughout the atmosphere were more valuable. With the publication of the Report also came personal attacks on some of the IPCC scientists which were to alert the scientific community to the kind of mud-flinging the skeptics were capable of (see box: Man in the middle).

In March 1996 the European scientific community were alerted to the formation of a skeptical group on their doorstep – the European Science and Environment Forum (ESEF). This group criticized the IPCC summaries for oversimplification of complex studies and complained that 'Any benefit of climate change is usually ignored in favor of pessimistic visions.'[1]

However, after the publication of the Second Assessment Report the issue of emissions reductions came to be firmly on the agenda at the Conference of Parties (COP) meetings of the Climate Change Convention. Despite clouds of disinformation the issue was not going away. In the US the fossil fuel lobby tried a variety of tactics from releasing alarming stories about outrageous energy bills if the status quo were disturbed to funding the teaching of 'how petroleum improves the quality of life' to schoolchildren.[4]

As the reality of climate change became more difficult to deny scientifically and with the Global Climate Coalition's dirty tactics coming under increasing scrutiny, the US subsidiary of British Petroleum (BP) withdrew from the group in October 1996, with Shell

Man in the middle

When the UN's Intergovernmental Panel on Climate Change (IPCC) was working on its Second Assessment Report in 1995, the industry-funded skeptics were unable to provide any compelling evidence to disprove the Report's findings. However, they picked their chance by rounding on Dr Benjamin Santer who had been given the task of making changes to the text so that it would match the wording of the summary more closely. The summary itself had emerged after much debate and wrangling.

In May, a month before the print version of the report appeared, Santer addressed a symposium with another IPCC scientist explaining the findings of the IPCC and the workings of the climate models they had used to a capacity crowd. At the end of his presentation, William O'Keefe, chair of the Global Climate Coalition and Don Pearlman laid in with a barrage of accusations. Santer they said had secretly changed the IPCC report, excising any dissenting voices and references to scientific uncertainties. Santer and his colleague's replies that one section of the report had been moved so that the document would be more accessible and that the chapter had been written not by Santer alone but by 40 scientists and reviewed by another 60 was met with outright disbelief.

If Santer was shaken by this very public attack, there was worse to come. With the publication of the Report came attacks in *The Washington Times*, *The Wall Street Journal*, and *The New York Times*. Santer was accused of politically 'cleansing the underlying scientific report' and 'a most disturbing corruption of the peer review process'. The aim of these unsubstantiated reports was not just to isolate and attack Santer, but to discredit the Report itself. Santer sent a letter to each of the Report's authors apprising them of the allegations. 'I had hoped that any controversy regarding the 1995 IPCC Report would focus on the science itself, and not on the scientists. I guess I was being naive.' Several of the IPCC scientists wrote in defense of Santer's integrity to the papers including chair Bert Bolin who in a letter to *The Wall Street Journal* stated 'No one could have been more thorough and honest.'

After this bout of scandal-mongering Santer had to endure one further attack. Republican congressman Dana Rohrabacher decided to give his friends in the fossil fuel lobby a helping hand by writing to the Secretary of Energy pressing her to withdraw funding from the laboratory where Santer worked. ∎

The Heat is On, Ross Gelbspan, Perseus Books, Massachusetts 1998; *The Carbon War*, Jeremy Leggett, Penguin, 1999.

following two years later. In 1997 BP committed $1 billion to solar energy, while Shell allocated $500 million to renewable energy options. Such good news must be seen through the filter of business reality. It could be interpreted as these two giants finally catching a glimpse of a future in which fossil fuel had but a small role to play and getting in early in the race to develop viable alternative energy options. But there was no concomitant commitment to reducing the scale of their oil exploration and it would appear that these companies view alternative energy as a sideline to their major business. Environmental critics also derided the sums allocated – when taking into consideration the fact that US businesses alone spend $500 million each year in 'greenwashing' their image. They also noted that as the global oil industry has a turnover of over $2 billion each day, the sums Shell and BP had allocated seem not quite so considerable. Meanwhile the mileage they got out of portraying themselves as clean, green corporations was considerable.

Stalling strategies

In 1997 with an important meeting of the Climate Convention looming in Kyoto, Japan, with targets and timetables for reducing emissions of greenhouse gases on its agenda, stalling moves were being set in motion by a resolution in the US Congress. Co-sponsored by Senator Robert Byrd, a Democrat from the coal state of West Virginia, and Senator Chuck Hagel, a Republican from Nebraska, a state whose farmers would stand to lose much from climatic adversity, it proposed ruling out any action on the climate change issue by the US unless developing countries also 'participate meaningfully' in taking steps to reduce their greenhouse-gas emissions. This was an old bogey that was revived at precisely the time when it would do the most damage – months before representatives of the world's governments would be gathering to attempt to thrash out a deal on emissions reductions. It threw out the arguments about equity that had framed the convention in favor of naked self-interest. Byrd argued that if the US agreed to reduce emissions, industries and jobs would flow right into the developing countries if they didn't have similarly binding commitments from them. But with two-thirds of US emissions arising out of the building and transport sectors, it was unlikely these jobs were at risk of moving anywhere.

That left the one third which is emitted by industry, a sector which the government could buffer with incentives rewarding energy efficiency.[3] Hagel is perhaps the ultimate climate change skeptic who rejects the science behind the greenhouse effect outright, saying it is 'unproven historically – it doesn't make any sense', and who denies that temperatures worldwide have been rising, despite concrete evidence to the contrary. For Hagel, as for Byrd, the bottom line is about the impact emissions reductions could have on the engine of big business. Again and again the argument surfaces that economic growth cannot in any way be compromised by the threat of impending climate catastrophe, instilling a kind of wait and see mentality that plays right into the hands of the skeptics. Patrick Michaels and others of his ilk often argue that they will believe climate change is for real when they see conclusive proof – a bit like waiting to see the smoke coming out of the barrel of a gun before declaring that you've been shot.

Who pays the piper?

The close relationship between fossil fuel producers and US politics is seen as a major sticking point when it comes to making progress on enacting measures that would benefit the environment. ∎

Industry contributions to US political parties (in US $ millions)

	1998	1997	Democrats	Republicans
Mobil Oil	$6.16	$5.24	16%	84%
Exxon	$5.62	$5.21	12%	88%
Texaco	$4.23	$5.63	24%	76%
Shell Oil	$3.72	$2.94	26%	74%

'Industry fossils deny problem', Alternatives Journal, Spring 2000.

Whilst Byrd and Hagel could not be said to have acted from any sense of altruism, their actions possibly were not just about saving the American economy from an imagined threat. It's just possible that they might have been looking after themselves, what with Byrd having received $199,700 dollars in political contributions from fossil-fuel related industries in 1996 alone and Hagel totting up $148,000 that same year.[5] Of course the Byrd-Hagel Resolution could have been defeated by right-minded politicians, but as it turned out senators lined up to vote in favor. The suggestion that somehow Majority World countries would otherwise gain an 'unfair' advantage had done the trick.

Daphne Wysham, a researcher with the

Smokescreen

The World Bank's remit is the alleviation of poverty and the promotion of sustainable development. So it's understandable that about a fifth of its lending goes towards energy generation in poor countries. But if sustainability was really that high on its agenda it wouldn't be spending 25 times more money on fossil fuel related projects than it did on renewable energy ones. This, according to Washington-based researcher Daphne Wysham, is exactly what it did between 1992 and mid-1998. According to her research each dollar the World Bank pays out to fossil fuel projects attracts up to five to six more in private investments. World Bank supported projects in Nigeria and Chad have encouraged the export of fuel to wealthy countries. When fossil fuel projects generate power in the home country it is usually allocated to urbanites and industry, including energy-hungry industries such as aluminum production, which often move in from other countries as soon as cheap energy becomes available. The rural poor usually remain unaffected by any benefit. Wysham reckons that 'nine out of ten energy projects financed by the World Bank benefit at least one corporation headquartered in the Group of 7 [rich] nations.'

In China, the World Bank spent $1.35 billion on building coal-fired power plants. Seeing as coal is the fuel that emits the largest amount of carbon dioxide per unit of energy produced it would appear that the World Bank cares little for its own sustainable development policies. In the coming decade the Bank has set aside only $50-100 million for renewable energy projects in China. As Kate Hampton, Wysham's colleague at the Sustainable Energy and Economy Network, points out, the US is the largest stakeholder in the World Bank, providing 18 per cent of its funds and could if it wanted, redirect its investments to China away from coal. In

Washington-based Institute for Policy Studies which has prepared several critical reports on World Bank involvement in fossil fuel projects, captured the mood in the US Senate when she said, 'Climate change is like the new Communism,' adding 'I've been told by people in the Treasury Department that we cannot mention the words climate change in our language [to Congress] in our appropriations for the World Bank; if we do it will be struck from the record.'[5]

With the Byrd-Hagel resolution still fresh, the Clinton administration, which had previously made noises that suggested some commitment to the issue of climate change and whose Vice-President Al Gore had once written an urgent call to action entitled

not doing so it can be seen as encouraging China to pollute.

Hampton writes, 'Given that it can meet 80 per cent of its investment requirements by domestic means and that it is not short of foreign transnationals vying for a share of the projected market, the Chinese power sector is hardly out with a begging bowl, in desperate need of scarce development dollars. The Government has more leverage than other recipient countries given that it is both a political and an economic priority for the West to keep China on the path to a market economy.

'Yet, the World Bank, which is supposed to provide finance to projects that would otherwise not garner funds, is squeezing out the private sector in China in its haste to appease the country. Major projects worth billions of dollars have gone ahead recently despite foreign assistance being withdrawn.

'...In terms of its total dollar amount, World Bank funding has been exceeded in the last two years by the fossil-fuel investments of some Chinese banks and private lenders from overseas. Nevertheless, the World Bank still plays a dominant role as an 'arranger', bringing together foreign investors, export credit agencies and the Chinese Government to realize energy investments – it remains the most important multilateral institution. In this role, the World Bank could be instrumental in directing new investments away from fossil fuels and towards energy efficiency and renewable energy. Instead it continues to pour billions into bringing about climate disaster while ignoring the plight of the majority of the Chinese population still living below the poverty line.' ■

From 'Smokescreen', Kate Hampton, *New Internationalist*, December 1999; 'The World Bank: Funding Climate Chaos', Daphne Wysham, *The Ecologist*, March/April 1999.

The politics of climate change

Earth in the Balance, seemed in a decidedly wobbly state to make any positive headway on the issue of emissions reductions. In 1992 Gore wrote 'Minor shifts in policy, marginal adjustments in ongoing programs, moderate improvements in laws and regulations, rhetoric offered in lieu of genuine change – these are all forms of appeasement designed to satisfy the public's desire to believe that sacrifice, struggle and a wrenching transformation of society will not be necessary.' Now it was time for the US delegation to Kyoto to play just that kind of dodging game that Gore had so eloquently condemned. And they were not the only country playing it. But it appeared that the views that the American delegation was to express at the Kyoto Conference were not the views of ordinary Americans who were increasingly making the connections between tornadoes, droughts, weird overnight epi-

The finger of blame

Historically, industrialized countries have contributed up to 90 per cent of the greenhouse gases that are tipping the world's weather system out of joint. Today, the US, with 4 per cent of world population, emits nearly a quarter of all greenhouse gases – equal to that of the entire Majority World, which has 80 per cent of world population.

This graph shows the per capita amount of **carbon** sent into the atmosphere by various countries and regions. However the per capita figure for **carbon dioxide** emissions is much higher, with each person in North America averaging 19 tonnes*. ∎

* US ton = 2,000 lbs.
1 metric tonne = 2,240 lbs/
1,000 kg.

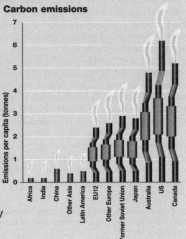

Carbon emissions

'Justice, Equity and Efficiency in Climate Change: A developing country perspective', P R Shukla in *Fair Weather? Equity Concerns in Climate Changes*, ed. Ferenc L Tóth, Earthscan 1999.

demics, explosions in the insect and rodent populations and the weather. For on the eve of the conference the *New York Times* published the results of a large opinion poll on Global warming – 65 per cent of the people polled felt that the US should cut its emissions immediately regardless of the position of other countries.

Division in Kyoto

As the Kyoto conference opened, the country positions seemed more or less clear from the outset. The view of the OPEC (oil-producing) countries, which had the most to lose, was that any emissions reduction target should be a low one. These oil-producers of the Middle East, fully briefed by the skeptics, set their faces firmly against any cuts that would threaten their livelihoods. Britain, where political behavior was showing some signs of moving beyond empty rhetoric, with Germany led the European call for cuts. However Iceland, with vast reserves of natural gas, and Norway with its North Sea oil reserves were notable dissenters arguing for an expansion of their emissions limits. Canada, whose per capita emissions are the second-highest, toed the US line of asking for parallel commitments from the developing world and Australia, the world's largest coal exporter, argued for an increase in its emissions. The industrializing nations were keen to defend their right to develop.

The strongest cuts in emissions were proposed by the Alliance of Small Island States whose member countries are at risk of sinking under rising seas, arguing for cuts of 20 per cent below 1990 levels, the baseline year agreed at Rio. Ambassador H E Tuiloma Neroni Slade of Samoa spoke with passion: 'The strongest human instinct is not greed – it is not sloth, it is not complacency – it is survival... and we will not allow some to barter our homelands, our people, and our culture for short-term economic interest.' But that did not prevent some countries suggesting that it would be cheaper to relocate the populations of some of these smaller island states than do something about emissions, a suggestion decried by the Prime Minister of Tuvalu as 'utterly insensitive and irresponsible'.

Predictably much of the wrangling was duplicitous in the extreme. OPEC members such as Saudi Arabia and Kuwait and their industry counterparts stuck to their line of trying to persuade large developing nations like India and China that climate change was just a scare, a plot of the wealthy countries to keep them poor. On the other hand they made it clear that they themselves would accept no cuts unless similar cuts were imposed on developing nations as well.[1] China had been visited by Exxon Chief Executive Lee Raymond little over a month earlier, who in his address to the World Petroleum Congress in Beijing did a hatchet job on the idea of global warming and encouraged China to exploit its fossil fuels to the fullest in order to achieve economic progress. Back in Washington Exxon had been financing the Global Climate Coalition's campaign that developing countries must commit to cuts at Kyoto.[3]

When the US and Canada insisted upon Majority World countries pledging reductions Zhong Shukong, the Chinese delegation leader, replied: 'In the developed world only two people ride in a car and you want us to give up riding the bus!' He was right: Los Angeles alone has more cars than the whole of China. Indeed if one were to look at the resource-guzzling indulged in by the wealthy world, it is clear that the West is in no position to waggle a finger at the comparatively thrifty South.

Commitments to change

Out of this tangle of positions and despite the best efforts of the industry-fueled skeptics emerged a target commitment from the wealthy countries of the world to cut their greenhouse gas emissions by 5.2 per cent below 1990 levels by 2010. In terms of effects on the world's temperature this would mean a mere 0.2° F (0.1° C) improvement in the projected warming of 2.7° F (1.5° C) over the coming 50 years according to the IPCC models.[6] Australia, Iceland and Norway were the exceptions winning increases in their emissions targets. The US committed itself to a 7 per cent cut while the EU target was 8 per cent. Even though the overall target was a far cry from the 50-70 per cent reductions that are needed to stabilize world climate and which would mean in effect a phasing out of fossil fuels, it was still an improvement on the business-as-usual scenario where emissions would be allowed to grow unchecked.

Kyoto was widely perceived at the time as a beginning whatever the disappointments over low targets. But three years down the line and with the IPCC's impending Third Assessment Report promising further confirmation of anthropogenic climate change in the offing, little has been done to meet even these targets. At the time of writing, of the 23 countries that have ratified the Kyoto Protocol none are industrialized nations with emissions reductions targets. Some sign of hope comes from the Bonn conference of 1999

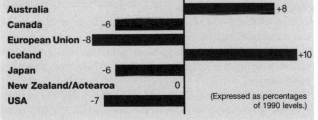

Low commitments

After the 1997 climate conference in Kyoto, the industrialized countries of the world made a commitment to cutting their greenhouse gas emissions which averaged at 5.2 per cent below 1990 levels. This was nowhere near the 50-70 per cent cuts needed, but was viewed at the time as a start.

Greenhouse gas emissions commitments of selected countries under the 1997 Kyoto Protocol.

Australia	+8
Canada	-6
European Union	-8
Iceland	+10
Japan	-6
New Zealand/Aotearoa	0
USA	-7

(Expressed as percentages of 1990 levels.)

where a larger number of nations made commitments to ratify in time for the convention to enter into force by 2002.

President Clinton did not dare to utter a squeak about ratification in a Republican-dominated Congress, and one wonders if his successor will fare any better. Indeed oil has played a significant part in George W Bush's checkered career and he has made no secret of his opposition to the modest limits set at Kyoto. His response to the problem of global warming sounds uncomfortably close to that of the fossil fuel lobby – apparently he thinks the matter needs 'more research'.

Loopholes: old habits die hard

The industrialized world's politicians have been busily studying how best to use the loopholes which they had created in the Kyoto Protocol that would allow them to carry on business as usual whilst making claims to doing something about the environment.

The US was instrumental in pushing through an Article in Kyoto that allows it and other industrialized countries that may have difficulty meeting their targets to trade emissions with countries that have generous targets. Cases in question are Russia and Ukraine, which since the collapse of their economics are already down on their 1990 levels of emissions. They were allowed increases of 50 and 120 per cent respectively under the Kyoto Protocol but it is highly unlikely that they would be able to use them. At this point companies in foreign countries could offer to buy some of their permissible emissions in order to carry on polluting without check. Since the emissions allowance was a theoretical increase anyway, such trading actually translates it into an actual increase in emissions whilst letting the purchaser claim they are meeting their targets.

Another bone of contention is the possible unlimited use of carbon sinks in the accounting; this could mean that countries do nothing to actually reduce fossil fuel emissions. Such sinks are primarily seen to be the planting of new forests, but the creative accounting involved is crazy. The use of sinks could actually encourage cutting down old growth forests in order to gain carbon credits from ecologically disastrous fast-growing monoculture plantations or genetically engineered tree species.[7] Those in favor include Canada, Japan, Australia, the US, New Zealand, Sweden and France.[8] Countries could invest in such sinks outside their own shores and still claim the credit.

Yet another loophole is the provision of emissions-reduction technologies to countries that cannot afford them and claim the emissions cut in pollution in the home country, the so-called Clean Development Mechanism. When the US and Canada argued that developing countries needed to make commitments of their own, they used it as a justification for dragging their heels over the issue. With this loophole they would enable some emissions reductions (and quite possibly lucrative contracts for the alternative energy industry riding piggyback on such gifts) in the Majority World and themselves gain the right to pollute more. US President Clinton attempted to put this into practice on a visit to India in 2000. Kathleen McGinty, Clinton's environmental policy advisor for ten years and chair of the White House council for environmental quality had stationed herself at an Indian research institution beforehand along with her husband Karl Hausker, a former senior official in the US Senate and the Environmental Protection Agency. What these high-level members of the Clinton administration were doing in Delhi soon became clear when McGinty began making a series of public speeches to Indian industrialists and members of the NGO community, trying to convince them that the Clean Development Mechanism would bring them great prosperity. This laid the ground for Clinton to broach the subject with the Indian Government. Unfortunately for him the Indian Prime Minister, aware of what was at stake, did not bite.[9]

In June 2000 a global coalition of environmental organizations including Greenpeace, World Wildlife Fund (WWF) and Friends of the Earth (FoE) voiced their concern that the 5 per cent reduction promised by the industrialized nations was in danger of being twisted to a 15 to 20 per cent increase, singling out the US, Canada, Japan, Australia and New Zealand as the 'main culprits'. Bill Hare, the Climate Policy Director of Greenpeace International, was particularly withering: 'These governments are trying to create the impression that they are moving ahead on climate policies while in reality, in the smoke-filled back-rooms of these negotiations [in Bonn, June 2000], they are systematically attempting to shred every last bit of environmental integrity from the Kyoto Protocol.'[8] To the European Union's credit it has been opposing the US over the loopholes issue, pushing for real reductions, though some commentators believe that this is yet another attempt to be seen to be green.

Rising emissions

So what then has been achieved aside from the hot air? Australia, allowed a generous 8 per cent increase under the Kyoto Protocol, has actually seen its emissions rise to 17 per cent over 1990 levels. The US looked set to be 30 per cent up from 1990 levels by 2010. The outlook for Canada was even more staggering, with official forecasts predicting a 130 per cent rise in emissions on 1990 levels by 2010 instead of the 6 per cent cut agreed at Kyoto.[10] A US think-tank, the Pew Center for Global Climate Change, reported that of the European countries it had studied only Britain was on track, while Germany would miss its target by 4 per cent (though its target was a high 25 per cent in the first place) and the Netherlands was up 17 per cent.[11] The Pew Center then proceeded to kick up a storm amongst environmental groups by suggesting that targets and timetables agreed at Kyoto ought to be renegotiated to 'realistic' levels. The Global Climate Coalition was happy to agree.[12]

A report in the *Financial Times* offered another, equally depressing, position. 'Henry Jacoby of the Massachusetts Institute of Technology, suggests another alternative: maintaining the Kyoto Protocol as a "useful facade". Even if the Protocol does not enter into force, negotiations could continue and countries take actions on climate change in a manner that suits their local political conditions.'[13] Talk about parallel realities.

Just how big a facade the Kyoto Protocol was in danger of becoming was revealed at the Sixth Conference of Parties (COP 6) conference at the Hague in the Netherlands during November 2000. With the Gore versus Bush ding-dong battle for the White House playing out back home, the US delegation arrived intent on clinging to the loopholes which it was the Conference's purpose to close. Right from the start American negotiators fielded searching questions by the world's media with an oleagenous slickness, insisting that a deal would be made and genuine compromises offered without budging from their position that their seven-per-cent Kyoto target would only be met by accounting for 'sinking' or absorption by forests and not plowing farmland.

Frank Loy, one of the US negotiators, stated he would do nothing that would 'jeopardize the American lifestyle' and advanced the hard-line economic argument that the Majority World's interests would be best served by an expanding US economy. Although it was the US position that finally led to the collapse of the talks, Japan and Canada were two other important players who were riding on the US delegation's coat-tails.

The flaw in the US argument was that the sinks they

were insisting on could not be proven to absorb a calculable percentage of emissions. The idea had met resistance from green commentators because it allowed polluters to claim reductions and meet targets simply by planting trees. At the Hague it ran into trouble with the European Union group of nations as well who were determined to preserve some semblance of environmental integrity for the Kyoto Protocol.

As deliberations wore on without any sign of a breakthrough and the conference overshot its closing deadline, British Deputy Prime Minister John Prescott received permission to undertake some last minute horse-trading with the US delegation. After a series of discussions that lasted through the night, he returned with a deal that contained little by way of real compromise from the US team. It was a rerun of previous negotiations where delaying tactics and the exhaustion

Fighting talk

Over the years leaders of small island nations have voiced their alarm and their objections to complacent politicians elsewhere with great eloquence. They are, after all, making a plea for their very survival. In the Maldives for example, which is particularly susceptible to sea level rise, President Maumoon Abdul Gayoom has been fighting his corner for years.

'It is in the interest of all the world that climatic changes are understood and the risks of irreversible damage to natural systems, and the threats to the very survival of man, be evaluated and allayed with the greatest urgency... it is not too late to save the world. It is not too late to save the Maldives...We did not contribute to the impending catastrophe to our nation; and, alone we cannot save ourselves.'
19 October 1987

'The North and the South must work out now an effective timetable for stabilizing and reducing atmospheric greenhouse gas concentrations and conserving global biodiversity – goals that are vital for the ultimate good of all human beings and life on Earth.'
12 June 1992

'So let me say this to the world: Watch what happens to us, the small island states. The threats that we face today will not be limited to us alone... Whatever our fate tomorrow, will be your fate the day after.'
27 March 1995

of delegates were used to push watered down agreements through.

This time though, with the IPCC's Third Assessment Report confirming that human activities had contributed substantially to global warming being widely leaked and new evidence before the delegates that temperatures could rise by a catastrophic upper limit of 10.8° F (6° C), the European Union delegation was in no mood to buy yet another compromise. Some NGO commentators are of the opinion that after the necessary numbers had been crunched Prescott's deal with the US would have led to actual emissions increases of between 6 and 9 per cent rather than any cuts. The Dutch Environment Minister Jan Pronk who chaired the conference had no other option but to let it close without any agreement. In a supreme irony, the conference center where COP 6 took place had to be made ready immediately for an oil industry exhibition that had been booked in to follow it.

Reflecting the bitter disappointment of the activist community which had maintained a very visible presence both within and outside the conference center, Tony Juniper of Friends of the Earth UK declared, 'No words can truly express our anger at what has happened here, or our sadness for the victims of climate change that is to come. The world will pay the price in tears.' The affair had also caused division between some US environmental groups who argued that the US proposals were the best chance yet of a deal and their counterparts from around the world, but especially Europe.

Many European activists felt, despite their disappointment, that the failure of the talks was preferable to a worthless deal which they would have been hard-pressed to support. Also for once the EU had refused to submit to what they considered the US's bullying tactics. This they felt would make for a stronger position in future negotiations. There were also calls to proceed with action on climate change regardless of

the US position, isolating it as the world's greatest pol-
luter in the global political community.

An issue that's here to stay

It is ironic that despite the abysmal political response,
the profile of the climate change issue is higher in
public perception than ever before. This is in part due
to the tireless efforts of environmental groups who
have been vocal and creative in their protests and who
have been key disseminators of information. It is in
part due to scientists who are increasingly appearing
on public and media platforms to warn of the dangers
and who have often been the most eloquent voices in
the argument for equitable political solutions to the
problem. And it is in quite considerable part due to
the weather itself as it continues to throw surprises
worldwide with each passing month.

A BBC television news report covering the worst
floods in the south east of England for 40 years in
November 2000 explicitly mentioned global warming
as the cause.[14] Parts of Britain are now twice as likely to
flood when compared to a few decades ago, and flooding events are expected to further intensify.

Some skeptics are beginning to change their minds,
whilst others are changing their tack from outright
denial of global warming to pleading that economic
imperatives require a cautious approach to the issue.
Some of the theories that they held – such as sunspots
being responsible for the recent warming – are being
conclusively disproved, in this case by their originator.
Following the recent US drought Republican Senator
John McCain found himself waking up to the issue as
scientist after scientist (including one who had previously voiced skeptical views) testified before a Senate
Commerce Committee that humankind was causing
global warming. McCain who had gone on the campaign trail, but failed to win nomination for the
presidential election, was also impressed by public concern. 'In town-hall meeting after town-hall meeting,

young people would stand up and say: "What is your position on global warming?"[15]

Meanwhile over at denial central, the Global Climate Coalition, the exodus continues with Texaco, The Southern Company, Ford, DaimlerChrysler and General Motors bailing out. How far this is because these corporations have seen the light is questionable. Mia Walton, a spokesperson for General Motors said their move was in order 'to take a global, holistic, more "GM" approach to the issue' of climate change, but reiterated her company's opposition to the Kyoto Protocol. It could be that companies are eager to distance themselves from the villainous image that the Global Climate Coalition has acquired, safe in the knowledge of the political stalemate.[16]

But in many quarters public greenhouse denial still continues unrepentant. Lee Raymond, chair of Exxon Mobil, addressed his corporation's annual meeting in typical devil-may-care style by asserting that the link between climate change and the burning of fossil fuels had not been proven. In his defense he cited a petition signed by "17,000" scientists'. However, the petition in question turned out to be an Internet sign-in with names including those of the Spice Girls and the cast of the film M*A*S*H*.[11]

European fuel protests

Whilst the dismal antics of politicians and corporate players may be easy targets, events across many European countries late in the summer of 2000 left me wondering just how genuine public concern really was. Starting with dock blockades by fishers in France over the price of diesel, protests soon spread to blockades on the roads and around petrol stations with truckers complaining over the cost of fuel. With the French government bowing to the protests within days, truckers and businesses whose profits depend upon cheap road transport in Britain began wondering what the French who paid much less for their fuel were up in arms about. Seeing the success of the French protests and the public sympathy they generated, trucks began drawing up at the gates of fuel depots in Britain to stop supplies from leaving.

Convoys began crawling down the highways with tailbacks stretching for miles crawling behind them. Within days, aided by a rash of panic buying, fuel began running out and public services started feeling the pinch. Throughout this period television news reporters questioned people queuing up at filling stations about their views on the strike. Most replied that the truckers had a point, fuel was far too expensive and the disruption of the country was worth it if it succeeded in getting the government to back down over taxes on fuel.

With images from the British strike playing across their television screens the protests spread to Belgium, the Netherlands, Germany, and parts of Scandinavia but on a smaller scale.

With normal life in Britain grinding to a halt within a week, the environmental voices seemed muted in this crisis. People were claiming cheaper fuel as if it were their birthright and glowed with a puritanical zeal in their quest for it. Britain had committed itself to progressive escalating taxation on fuel in 1993 as an environmental measure. (The Clinton administration had proposed a carbon tax, but it was pulled in after the predictably hostile Congress reaction to it.) This tax designed to pay an environmental dividend, was also intended to cut down on car use. Why were people then so bitterly against it? Were they failing to make the connections when it boiled down to a question of cash? Were they in fact showing the same kinds of priorities that big business had shown on a global scale?

The situation, however, was somewhat more complex than that. When the fuel protests had been called off, environmentalists claimed that they had had plenty to say, but had been filtered out by the news media that were happy to chase the story of a major protest slowly paralyzing the nation. It was obvious the tax had been hitting some people in rural areas and small businesses hard, but that was because the British government had done little to introduce compensatory mechanisms such as affordable, efficient public transport. Little had been done to reverse the trend of out of town superstores which had devastated shops on high streets and left people with no option but to drive great distances to do their shopping. Factories, warehouses and offices were all being located in places which meant workers had to drive further all the time.

A letter to *The Independent* newspaper chastised the automobile industry for promoting an oil dependent culture. 'The issue exercising fuel protesters should not be the price of fuel, but the price of travel. Their anger would be better directed at the car manufacturers who have had every opportunity since the first oil crisis in the 1970s to design lightweight and fuel-efficient vehicles using alternative propulsion systems to the criminally inefficient internal combustion engine (typical output of useful energy: 10 to 15 per cent of input).'[17]

Need and greed

And yet, despite such valid arguments the niggling thought persisted that the kinds of instant-gratification high-consumption lifestyles people had got accustomed to, driving large distances without a second thought, had as large a part to play in the protests. If the protests were about need, then they were also in many cases about greed. Alongside the legitimate arguments there was also a place for the kind of short-sightedness that had plagued the delegates at Kyoto.

Another letter recounted the state of the nation: 'It was alarming to see a "developed" country being reduced to hoarders and panic-buyers within a week. With theft of other drivers' petrol and fights apparently breaking out in supermarkets over bulk-buying of food staples, it seems that civilization is a very thin veneer.'[18]

All this came after a few days of protest. What the reaction would be to the grave ructions of climatic crises is anybody's guess.

1 *The Heat is On*, Ross Gelbspan, Perseus Books, Massachusetts 1998. **2** 'Cry foul, cry freedom', *New Internationalist*, April 1990. **3** *The Carbon War*, Jeremy Leggett, Penguin, London 1999. **4** Christian Huot, unpublished report for the *New Internationalist*, 1999. **5** 'How US Politics is Letting the World Down', Simon Retallack, *The Ecologist*, March/April 1999. **6** *The Breakdown of Climate*, Peter Bunyard, Floris Books, Edinburgh 1999. **7** 'Time to close the forests and climate loopholes', World Wildlife Fund (WWF) press release, 10 May, 2000. **8** 'Kyoto climate treaty off course, heading for the rocks', WWF press release, 13 June, 2000. **9** 'Spreading myths of money', Anju Sharma, *Down to Earth*, 15 April, 2000. **10** 'Mind the Gap', Ralph D Torrie and Richard Parfett, *Alternatives Journal*, Spring 2000. **11** *The Cutting Edge*, No 5, WWF, 2000. **12** 'Emissions targets "unrealistic" says US climate change body', Colin Macilwain, *Nature*, 27 July, 2000. **13** 'Vital talks loom in the Hague', Vanessa Houlder, *Financial Times*, 29 September, 2000. **14** BBC News, 12 November 2000. **15** 'Congress wakes up to climate change', Colin Macilwain, *Nature*, 25 May, 2000. **16** 'Car-maker joins exodus from anti-Kyoto coalition', Meredith Wadman, *Nature*, 23 March, 2000. **17** Dr Jane Roberts, Letter to *The Independent*, 19 September, 2000. **18** Dorothy Hutton, Letter to *The Independent*, 16 September, 2000.

7 Lasting solutions for a global crisis

How much more carbon can we send into the atmosphere... the argument for sustainability and equitable solutions... not all renewable energy is clean... a wealth of energy options... efficiency for a change.

'EXPLOIT OR EXPLORE?' asks the two-page advertisement staring at me from *Time* magazine. One half of the page is monochrome and a bulldozer plows through the carnage of lush vegetation. Over it hovers the ghostly outline of the Shell logo. The other side of the page is a burst of green – trees, ferns, calla lilies sprawl across it, evocative of Eden. Over this picture, which has the kind of unreal beauty common to photographs of dishes in certain kinds of cookbooks, is stamped the Shell logo in full color.

The advertising copy does its best to suggest a caring, sharing transnational. 'Our shared climate and finite natural resources concern us as never before, and there's no room for an attitude of "It's in the middle of nowhere, so who's to know?"' asserts the advert.

'If we're exploring for oil and gas reserves in sensitive areas of the world, we consult widely with the different local and global interest groups. Working together, our aim is to ensure that bio-diversity in each location is preserved. We also try to encourage these groups to monitor our progress so that we can review and improve the ways in which we work.' To stop me wondering if I'm dreaming there's also a television advertisement, with a photogenic female Earth scientist projecting the caring hands-on line in a tropical forest location. We're supposed to trust her, she isn't a man in a suit; she would do right by the world.

Well, only if anyone was gullible enough to believe it. Shell doled out $200,000 to environmental groups with maximum publicity to demonstrate its good intentions. Or was it to draw public attention away from its well-documented abuses of the environment and the Ogoni people in Nigeria and the PR disaster that was Brent Spar?

An alternative take on Shell's fantasia was proposed in an article in *Red Pepper* magazine: 'Oil spills caused by either sabotage or neglect are reported at least twice a week in Nigeria. Hundreds of hectares of forest are dead. Pools of crude oil stretch in every direction. Several thousand people have died over recent years through oil fires and pipeline ruptures. Yet, last year [1999], Shell spent £32 million on cleaning up its image as opposed to cleaning up the mess it has made in Nigeria.'[1]

Along with Shell, British Petroleum (BP) is another oil giant that has trumpeted its green credentials lately, playing up its investment in solar energy and changing its logo to resemble a sunburst. BP we are told no longer stands for British Petroleum but Beyond Petroleum. If only this were true. However, 99.9 per cent of BP's energy investment remains in fossil fuels. In its year 2000 AGM, BP Amoco's own shareholders voiced concern over Northstar, its new Arctic oil field. As many as 13.5 per cent of them voted to abandon oil production in this ecologically fragile region and a redirection of those funds to BP's solar subsidiary.[2] Although by no means anywhere near a majority this still represents a significant chunk of shareholders in what is essentially a fossil fuel company.

In early August, six Greenpeace activists boarded a giant BP barge off the coast of Alaska to protest against this development. Stephanie Tunmore, one of the six, made her views on BP's greenwash quite clear: 'BP, who claim to be on the side of the climate, are actually doing everything they can to perpetuate climate change.'

Both Shell and BP are criticized by environmental organizations like Greenpeace because their investments in alternative forms of energy are not being met with corresponding cuts in their fossil fuel exploration and exploitation activities. In the light of this, their forays into solar energy look like little more than cynical attempts to get in ahead of the game. They seem to be waiting before making serious investment until the time is right to make a killing – when the market for solar energy, already expanding rapidly, takes off.

If, as is often argued, this is only the economic imperative doing its thing, then attention needs to be drawn to the larger reality of the ecological imperative. Economies are part of ecological systems and not above them, a message that business leaders don't seem to want to hear. But the arguments are being made with compelling eloquence by both climate scientists and environmental activists.

Carbon budget

In 1997 Greenpeace put forward the idea of a 'carbon budget' – the amount of fossil fuels that could safely be burnt in order to stabilize world climate. They calculated this working with limits of temperature change set by the United Nations Advisory Group on Greenhouse Gases, which estimated that the outer limits for temperature change to which the Earth could adapt were 0.2° Fahrenheit (0.1° Celsius) per decade, with a maximum tolerable increase of 1.8° F (1° C). Beyond this latter limit, the UN group had predicted that the Earth's response to the temperature signal would be 'rapid, unpredictable and non-linear' leading to widespread ecosystem damage. The closing decades of the 20th century have outstripped the decadal upper limits.

Keeping the 1.8° F (1° C) stabilization limit and the fact that the climatic effects of atmospheric carbon are delayed by 50 years or more in mind, Greenpeace calculated that the total amount of carbon that could be burnt was 225 billion tonnes*. If deforestation continued at current rates this would drop to 145 billion tonnes. But the more optimistic 225 billion tonnes figure itself accounts for just 5 per cent of estimated total fossil fuel resources. If we view it in terms of known economically viable reserves it is still only 25 per cent of the total amount. This is what is staring the fossil fuel companies in the face – the fact that 75 per cent of the reserves they have located would have to remain in the ground and any further exploration would have to stop.[3]

It is worthwhile here to look at emissions levels. Before industrialization, the atmospheric concentrations of carbon dioxide were pretty stable at 280 parts per million (ppm). Today they are 360 ppm and growing. If stabilization at this level were to be aimed at, it would require emissions cuts of around 70 per cent. If the target is stabilization at 450 ppm, then global emissions would have to start going down within the next few years, eventually plunging by well under 50 per cent of today's levels. A third concentration of 550 ppm – roughly double the pre-industrial figure – would still require eventual cuts of more than 50 per cent.

This range of scenarios demonstrates conclusively, that if the ultimate aim is the stabilization of carbon dioxide in the atmosphere at levels that will not fuel severe climate change, then a drastically low carbon future must be envisaged. For the 550 parts per million scenario is by no means a 'safe' one. Whilst alternative energy solutions abound, there is a deafening silence from policy researchers on the issue of low carbon futures. The emissions reductions targets set at Kyoto, whilst viewed as a beginning by the generously inclined, barely scratch the surface of the cuts required if atmospheric concentrations of greenhouse gases are to stop growing indefinitely.

Sustainability and equity

In many respects the climate change debate needs to bring the wider issues of sustainability and equity much more into its remit, rather than being focused

*1 US ton = 2,000 lbs. 1 metric tonne = 2,240 lbs/1,000 kg.

on the technicalities of emissions reductions, essential as they are. Here's why.

For decades now the West has pursued the mantra of economic growth at any cost. Increases in the gross domestic product (GDP), whether they be from the most polluting and resource-intensive industries or from the increased police activity of countering crime, have been viewed as 'growth'. This has led to a 'we consume because we can' mentality, which is straining the environmental resources of the Earth to its limits and has created chasms of inequality between nations.

Fossil fuel reserves set against the 'carbon budget'

The fossil fuel resources already located are far higher than Greenpeace's proposed carbon budget of 225 billion tonnes*. This carbon budget is the total amount of carbon that can be emitted into the atmosphere in the future by human activity without causing serious climate change. If steps are to be taken to address climate change, then it follows that many of these resources must not be exploited. ■

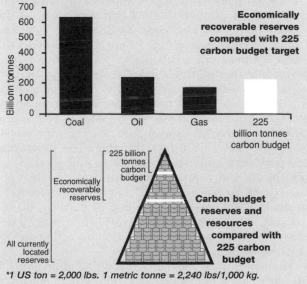

Economically recoverable reserves compared with 225 carbon budget target

Carbon budget reserves and resources compared with 225 carbon budget

*1 US ton = 2,000 lbs. 1 metric tonne = 2,240 lbs/1,000 kg.

Fossil Fuels and Climate Protection: The Carbon Logic, Greenpeace International, October 1997; Nature's Bottom Line: Climate Protection and the Carbon Logic, Greenpeace, May 1999.

One US citizen laid down the consumption record of her fellow Americans in these words:

'The United States comprises 5 per cent of Earth's population and consumes 25 per cent of its resources.

'It is deeply painful, as an American, to state this. Yet these are the facts. Americans use twice as much water as someone from a developing country. Americans use twice as much energy as someone from Germany, France or the United Kingdom; 50 times that of a Guatemalan, 100 times that of a Vietnamese and 500 times that of a person living in Chad. With 5 per cent of the global population, we consume 25 per cent of the planet's fossil fuels each year, emitting 20 per cent of its greenhouse gases. City dwellers in the US generate twice the amount of trash as their counterparts in Spain, Italy or Germany. The US produces ten times the amount of hazardous waste as the next largest producer.

'When we speak of transportation in America, we are speaking primarily of the automobile. Only 8 per cent of all of the people on Earth own a car. In the United States 89 per cent have at least one car. Working people spend nine hours a week behind the wheel – almost one-tenth of our waking moments... No people use air travel more than Americans, and plane travel consumes over six times more energy than traveling by car. Food production and consumption place enormous stress on the human as well as the planetary system. A typical American dinner travels over 1,000 miles from farm to table. The processing and packaging add substantial costs to the food (4 per cent of our per capita expenditure on all consumer goods goes for packaging – $225 per person a year)... In the last 200 years we have lost 50 per cent of our wetlands, 90 per cent of our old-growth forests, 99 per cent of the tall grass prairie and as many as 490 species of native plant and animal species.'[4]

The writer is no hair-shirted hippie but former US Congress member Claudine Schneider – and a

Republican to boot. The desecration of the planet is plain to see and there can be little doubt that vastly over-consuming lifestyles cannot be sustained indefinitely. In the Netherlands, despite the great cultural value associated with thrift, it is estimated that the average citizen would have to cut their consumption by a whopping 70 to 90 per cent in order to live within their environmental space.[5] Friends of the Earth Netherlands have estimated that one-and-a-half times the country's total land area is under forest *abroad*, just to supply it with its wood and paper needs.[6] This tiny densely-populated country has a purchasing power that is two-thirds that of India, a land 93 times its size. Whilst the Netherlands might have achieved much in terms of environmentally friendlier public policies it is a bit premature to talk in terms of the 'decoupling' of economic growth and environmental pressure.

Viewed in this light, the climate crisis is but one more manifestation of unsustainable growth, albeit one which could have devastating effects in the near future. If we are to build a future, where the threat to the environment could recede, sustainability must be a key consideration.

No level playing field

The equity argument follows on from the sustainability argument. There cannot be a level playing field in emissions reductions when there are such gross inequities in the wealth of nations. Much of this wealth has been derived from environmental degradation in the first place. Andrew Simms of the New Economics Foundation proposes that the industrialized world is in fact greatly indebted when environmental issues are brought to bear on conventional economics. 'The logic of a radical change of behavior, in the face of what is a huge environmental debt to the global community, should not be difficult to grasp in the industrialized world. The rich countries have been demanding for decades that very poor countries undergo massive change in response to much smaller financial debts... There is a direct link between fossil fuel use and economic output. Because of this, the carbon debt can be given illustrative values in economic efficiency terms. Such sums show the heavily indebted poor countries actually in carbon credit up to three times the value of their ordinary debts. The Group of Seven industrialized countries on the other hand, appears $13 trillion in debt.'[7]

An essential element of climate negotiations should be the recognition of this environmental indebtedness. This would allow for stricter emissions targets for industrialized countries and the massive transfer of clean technologies to developing countries, which would aid them in leapfrogging straight to sustainable, renewable energy in their quest for economic security. Such measures would require thinking that went beyond short-term national interests to hammer out a schedule of global governance that would ensure an equitable, sustainable, energy future. Any measures taken would also have to extend to the interests of nations whose economies are dependent on oil production, factoring in the wealth these nations may or may not have earned into the energy transition package.

In the normal run of things there is about as much chance of this happening as there is of pigs flying, but the alternative of global bullying does not work in climate negotiations. A rising tide of activist opinion is on the side of such solutions because they realize this is the true *realpolitik*, not the dodging and diving practiced by their politicians.

False alternatives

With the climate debate heating up, the alternative energy industry sees a rosy future ahead, joining the ranks of the fossil fuel transnationals and ultimately overtaking them. Many are already hearing the ring of cash registers as they contemplate the emerging markets of India, China and Eastern Europe. They

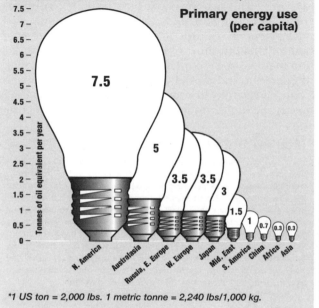

Power point

A quarter of the world's population – in the North – consumes more than 70 per cent of the world's commercial energy while the remaining three-quarters – in the South – consume less than 30 per cent. ■

Primary energy use (per capita)

Tonnes of oil equivalent per year

N. America 7.5
Australasia 5
Russia, E. Europe 3.5
W. Europe 3.5
Japan 3
Mid. East 1.5
S. America 1
China 0.7
Africa 0.3
Asia 0.3

*1 US ton = 2,000 lbs. 1 metric tonne = 2,240 lbs/1,000 kg.

'Renewable Energy and the Future', Peter Harper, paper, 1996

have visions of power, of becoming transnationals that could market technologies that are not tied to an extractable resource but to free wind and sunlight. Whilst the energy revolution could provide the alternative energy sector with a huge growth spurt, viewing developing countries purely as markets would wreck chances of emissions reductions. The means to develop alternative energy sources would have to be decoupled from ability to pay. Why else does China persist in exploiting its heavily polluting coal reserves causing health problems amongst its own people? It is because China and countries at a similar stage of industrialization don't have the infrastructure to make the leap to economically viable alternative sources of energy.

The natural gas and nuclear industries are vying to paint themselves as sources of clean energy. Whilst natural gas, with its lower carbon dioxide emissions, could have a small role to play as a transitional fuel, nuclear energy cannot seriously be considered as an option. First off, short of building a nuclear power station that had zero scope for error, which could remain in operation indefinitely, and was indestructible were a natural calamity like an earthquake to occur, there is no way the highly radioactive plutonium-rich fuel used

Making the sea bloom

Up until now human efforts at controlling the weather have been relatively small in scale. These have included cloud seeding in order to increase rainfall, firing silver iodide into hail clouds in order to reduce the size of hailstones and seeding thunderstorms with metallic chaff in an attempt to neutralize their electric fields. The jury's still out on whether these methods work. Gardeners have tried various tricks to attempt to control frost-damage to plants. Some of the more ingenious measures have included employing large fans to mix cold ground air with the warmer air a few meters up, spraying water which by freezing would release latent heat into the air, and using smoking smudge pots that slowly burn fuel over a period of time.

Recently however scientists have played with the idea of affecting climate on a larger scale. An international team led by Philip Boyd of New Zealand's University of Otago succeeded in creating a phytoplankton bloom over 90 miles (150 kilometers) long and 2 miles (4 kilometers) wide in the Southern Ocean by scattering over 18,000 pounds (8,500 kilograms) of iron salts in the water. They were acting on an idea mooted ten years earlier of boosting the sea's carbon dioxide absorption by promoting the growth of phytoplankton which draw the gas down from the atmosphere.

This artificially created bloom lasted for a month, but left little evidence that the carbon dioxide drawn down by phytoplankton had actually sunk to deeper waters, something that would need to happen if the aim is to create a permanent sink of the gas. However, other researchers pointed out that such efforts might result in the deoxygenation of deep sea waters and the creation of more potent greenhouse gases. Not an idea whose time has come, then. ■

Steve Connor *The Independent*, 13 October, 2000; 'Hail and high water', *New Internationalist*, December 1999.

could be considered safe. The waste product from such a plant would also need to be effectively sealed off for hundreds of years before it no longer posed a threat to human health. To take one recent example – the Dounreay nuclear plant on Scotland's northern coast will cost an estimated $8.7 billion (£6 billion) to shut down and the process will take at least 50 years. Even with all high-level radioactive waste removed from the plant it would still require monitoring for a further 300 years.[8]

Also moving out of the alternative sources of energy picture are hydroelectric projects involving reservoirs and dams. The dam builders have pushed hard for hydroelectricity to be included in the Kyoto Protocol's list of sustainable technologies. Long under attack from environmentalists and local communities for destroying homes and habitats, such projects also cannot claim to produce greener energy. The bad news is that reservoirs are leaking methane and carbon dioxide into the atmosphere, especially in the tropics where the submerged vegetation rots more rapidly.

Researchers from Canada, where some of the world's largest hydroelectric projects are located, claim that these are responsible for up to a fifth of all methane emissions and their total contribution to the anthropogenic greenhouse effect could be as high as seven per cent. At present it is believed that the third of the world's reservoirs that are located in tropical regions contribute 80 per cent of such emissions, but in the long run reservoirs in northern countries could begin to catch up. Reservoirs that have been built over peat bogs cause special concern as a thick peat bog could hold greater reserves of decomposable carbon than a rainforest.[9]

Staring at the sun

Each year the sun shines down the energy equivalent of 1,000 trillion barrels of oil.[10] The solar potential for energy production is at least 1,000 times more than the energy currently being used worldwide. Photovoltaic cells and panels which produce electricity directly from sunlight can enable a building to generate more electricity than it needs – this isn't science fiction, the technology already exists. In Britain it is estimated that a typical house fitted with solar panels would save up to 2.5 tonnes* of carbon dioxide emissions a year. Up until recently the silicon-based cells were relatively expensive to manufacture but Japanese technology has paved the way for super-thin cells that considerably save on raw materials. Costs are now down to less than a tenth of what they were 20 years ago. Germany aims to install 100,000 solar roofs by 2004 and the United States 1,000,000 by 2010.

Where funds have been available, Majority World countries have been quick to harness solar energy. In Mongolia some of the *gurs* (tents) of nomadic herding communities have solar panels parked outside them. Where there is sunlight there is solar energy to be had, and it doesn't have to be warm for them to work – in fact they are most efficient in colder temperatures and snow reflects additional light onto them. A single 40/60-watt solar module can provide a nomadic family with five hours light, and energy for a television and radio. In Eritrea, the Democratic Republic of Congo, Sudan, Uganda and other African countries solar power is being harnessed in areas remote from the electricity grid to keep medicines and vaccines cool in clinics.[11] In Kenya more rural households get their electricity from solar energy than from the national grid.

Large-scale solar generation has remained a pipe dream, however, with critics claiming such energy would be more expensive. But with no major effort made so far to build a large enough plant that would generate enough power to lower unit costs, this argument runs hollow. As solar champion Jeremy Leggett put it: 'How much would it cost to build a price-bust-

*1 US ton = 2,000 lbs. 1 metric tonne = 2,240 lbs/1,000 kg.

Solar harvest

The sun can produce at least 1,000 times more usable energy than we currently need.
- In OECD – or Western industrialized countries – the usable solar harvest is 170 times more than needed
- In the CIS – former USSR countries – the ratio is 400
- In the South – or Majority World – it is 950
- If solar photovoltaic cells (which produce electricity from sunlight) were deployed wholesale today in homes and offices, they could generate two-thirds of the UK's current production each year. ■

OECD: 170 x need

CIS: 400 x need

MW: 950 x need

Unlocking the Power of our Cities, Greenpeace, London 1995.

ing plant? The answer is about $100 million. A single oil rig can set you back $4,000 million these days. We are talking about less than a leg off an oil rig to show the world that electricity can be generated by the sun as cheaply as it can by burning fossil fuel, pretty much anywhere we want it, even in cloudy latitudes.'[12]

Other systems of solar technology use the sun's energy to directly heat water – all new buildings in Israel are required to have such installations, cutting the country's fuel imports by five per cent.

The wind and the waves

Solar is by no means the only clean energy source. Windmills have been used to pump water and grind grain in Holland for hundreds of years. Today though, Dutch farmers are encouraged to invest in wind turbines that catch the wind's energy with their propeller-like blades and turn it into electricity by mechanically spinning a generator. Any excess electricity can be sold back to the national grid.

Wind power is economic as well as ecological, because once the initial costs of the turbine are covered, running costs are quite low. It can also reach areas where the outlay for conventional power lines connected to a central grid would be prohibitive. A southern Indian wind farm with 2,000 turbines is the second largest in the world and China aims to be producing eight million kilowatts of wind power by 2020. It has been estimated that Britain has the largest off-shore wind resource in Europe, capable of generating three times the nation's electricity requirements. Greenpeace UK calculates that if Britain made the commitment over the coming decade to generating 10 per cent of its electricity from this source it could lead to the creation of 30,000 new jobs.

Whereas large-scale dams and reservoirs cannot figure in the clean energy equation, micro-hydro projects that channel smaller bodies of water through turbines could still go some distance towards solving the energy needs of smaller communities. The oceans could be tapped both for thermal energy and the mechanical energy of tides, which could be converted into electricity.

The worldwide potential for wave power is gigantic, with ideal locations for tidal power stations along the western coasts of Europe and the US, the coasts of New Zealand and Japan. Energy could be generated by placing bell-like structures in the sea, which when the waves entered or left them would expel or pull in air through a turbine located at the top the structure. The movement of the turbine would generate electricity. Tidal barrages at the sea mouth or in rivers could gather water at high tide allowing it to flow back through a power-generating turbine when the tide moved out or river levels fell.

There are a number of replacement fuels waiting in

the wings to take over from oil and coal that could help cut emissions. Biogas, which comes from farmyard waste and burns relatively cleanly is being used by Indian and Vietnamese farmers.

Hydrogen derived from water is the cleanest fuel of all and could power homes as well as cars. Hydrogen gas combines with oxygen in a fuel cell to produce energy. Its waste products are heat that could be used for heating purposes and water. Ford has already thrown $1 billion at a zero-emissions car that uses a hydrogen fuel cell. The electricity required for isolating the hydrogen could be derived from renewable sources. Sadly this is not the plan of the big oil companies who are gearing up to produce it from natural gas.

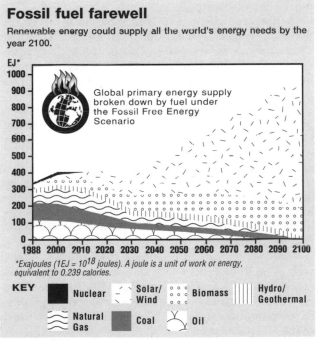

Fossil fuel farewell

Renewable energy could supply all the world's energy needs by the year 2100.

Global primary energy supply broken down by fuel under the Fossil Free Energy Scenario

*Exajoules (1EJ = 10^{18} joules). A joule is a unit of work or energy, equivalent to 0.239 calories.

KEY

Nuclear   Solar/Wind   Biomass   Hydro/Geothermal

Natural Gas   Coal   Oil

Greenpeace 1993

With such a multitude of energy options available –
and many of the technologies have been around for
decades crying out for further development – it seems
like nothing short of a death wish that governments
across the globe spend over $200 billion each year
subsidizing the fossil fuel industry. If such subsidies
could be diverted to clean, renewable energies along
with revenues from environmental taxes, the transformation in the energy scenario could be revolutionary.
In fact a group of environmental NGOs have estimated the cost of stabilizing global emissions of
greenhouse gases at $80 billion a year, far below what
fossil fuels receive.[13]

Efficiency

But while we're holding our breaths for the revolution, a bit of common sense may not go amiss. The
field of energy efficiency has massive emissions reductions and financial savings to offer. Former President
Clinton went on record as saying that a 20-per-cent
reduction in emissions could be achieved in the US
just by wasting less energy.[14] Other studies have put the
percentage even higher than that.

Efficient home building has often been a key feature
of temperature control in many poor warm countries
where there may either be no electricity or it may be too
expensive to use for cooling purposes. Courtyards at the
center of the house or cooling towers above them help
to lower temperatures without expending any energy.
Trees throwing shade onto walls keep them cooler.
Research on similar smart buildings in the Western
world suggests that architects need to pay more attention to simple things like access to sunlight in order to
save electricity costs in buildings. Commonsense ideas
such as building offices with an optimum depth so that
every desk has some access to daylight can lower light-
ing costs dramatically. The clever design of appliances
to use minimum amounts of energy can save two-thirds
of the electricity used.

Efficiency can also be extended in the sphere of public transport, such as the much-lauded integrated bus system in Curitiba, Brazil, which has lowered car use, reducing petrol consumption by 30 per cent. 70 per cent of Curitiba's citizens use buses.

The remarkable thing about efficiency is that a little goes a long way, so people can actually live better for less. At a personal level efficiency need not involve rocket science – it can be as simple as remembering to switch off all appliances that aren't being used or just reusing and recycling more.

The CMHC Canadian Housing Information Center has been calculating how simple energy savings translate into emissions reductions. Some of their findings are in the box below.[15]

There are answers enough from the tiniest to the grandest scale, ranging from the most basic technology to the most sophisticated, but they can never work within a global political framework that pays lip-service to sustainability and which has at its foundations colossal

Action – how we can cut emissions

Saving in pounds/kilograms of emissions reduction

Installing energy efficient light bulbs	55 pounds/25 kilograms/year for each frequently used bulb.
Replace appliances with highest efficiency models	880 pounds/400 kg/yr.
Wash clothes in cold water	496 pounds/225 kg/yr for each load per week
Turn down your thermostat 1°C/1.8°F	1,322 pounds/600 kg/yr for an average house
Reduce air travel	3,307 pounds/1,500 kg/yr for each 3,600 miles/6,000 kilometer trip avoided.
Reduce consumption	661 pounds/300 kg/yr for each garbage bag less put out each week.
Become vegetarian	981 pounds/445 kg/yr.
Buy locally produced seasonal produce	88 pounds/40 kg/yr.

inequity. Left to their own devices there seems to be little evidence that the politicians of some of the world's richest nations will do anything decisive. Here too, we have a mandate as individual citizens to call them to order. It will need a groundswell of ordinary citizens making their objections to the status quo plain in order to 'wrestle the Earth from fools' (as singer Patti Smith put it). The time to watch and wait has already run out. It's time to switch on the alternatives.

1 'The great greenwashed', Richard Gilpin and Ali Dale, *Red Pepper*, June 2000. **2** 'Shareholders vote against BP Arctic oil plans', *Positive News*, Summer 2000. **3** 'Nature's bottom line: Climate protection and the carbon logic', Greenpeace, May 1999. **4** 'Consumption: United States', Claudine Schneider, in *The Planetary Interest* edited by Kennedy Graham, UCL Press, London 1999. **5** 'The Netherlands' National Environmental Policy Plan', Resource Renewal Institute, 1988. **6** *Sustainable Netherlands Revisited*, Friends of the Earth Netherlands, 1996. **7** 'A climate of debt' by Andrew Simms, *Resurgence*, July/August 2000. **8** 'Nuclear plant will take 50 years to dismantle', Steve Connor, *The Independent*, 10 October, 2000. **9** 'Plumbing the depths of insanity', Fred Pearce, *The Independent*, 13 October, 2000. **10** *Climate change: Awareness and Action*, Dave Mussell, Juleta Severson-Baker and Tracey Diggins, Pembina Institute for Appropriate Development, Ottawa 1999. **11** 'Leapfrogging', Vanessa Baird, *New Internationalist*, October 1996. **12** 'Solar PV: Talisman for hope in the greenhouse', Jeremy Leggett, *The Ecologist*, March/April 1999. **13** *The Heat is On*, Ross Gelbspan, Perseus Books, Massachusetts 1998. **14** United Nations Associations of the USA website http://www.unuoa.org/programs/gcc.htm **15** *Alternatives Journal*, Spring 2000.

CONTACTS

International

Greenpeace International
Active in pressuring governments and industry to shift from dirty energy to renewables. A good source of documentation on climate change at the poles, coral reefs and 'carbon budgets'.
Keizersgracht 176
1016 DW Amsterdam
The Netherlands
Tel: + 31 20 523 6222
Fax: +3]1 20 523 6200
Website:
www.greenpeace.org/~climate

Friends of the Earth International Secretariat
Also in the frontline, lobbying for action on climate change.
PO Box 19199
1000 GD Amsterdam
The Netherlands
Tel: +31 20 6221369
Fax: +31 20 639281
E-mail: foei@foei.org
Website: www.foei.org

The Intergovernmental Panel on Climate Change can be contacted via
The IPCC Secretariat
World Meteorological Organization Building
7 bis Avenue de la Paix, CP 2300
CH-211 Geneva 2
Switzerland
Tel: +41 22 730 8208
Fax: +41 22 730 8025
E-mail: ipcc_sec@gateway.wmo.ch
Website: www.ipc.ch

The EarthAction Network consists of citizen groups in more than 150 countries and campaigns on a wide range of environmental issues.

In the UK contact:
EarthAction
17 The Green, Wye
Kent TN25 5AJ
Tel: +44 1233 813 796
Fax: +44 1233 813 795
E-mail: wye@earthaction.org.uk

In the US contact:
EarthAction
30 Cottage Street
Amherst, MA 01002
Tel: +1 413 549 8118
Fax: +1 413 549 0544
E-mail: amherst@earthaction.org
Website: www.earthaction.org

United Nations Environment Program
United Nations Avenue, Gigiri
PO Box 30552,
Nairobi, Kenya
Tel: + 254 2 621234
Fax: +254 2 624489/90
Website: www.unep.org

WWF International
Avenue du Mont-Blanc
CH-1196, Gland
Switzerland
Tel: +41 22 364 91 11
Fax: +41 22 364 53 58
Website: www.panda.org

Aotearoa / New Zealand

Greenpeace New Zealand
113 Valley Road
Mt Eden
Auckland
Tel: +64 9 630 6317
Fax: +64 9 630 7121
E-mail:
webmanager@nz.greenpeace.org

National Institute of Water and Atmosphere (NIWA)
PO Box 109-695
Newmarket
Auckland
Tel: +64 9 375 2090
Fax: +64 9 375 2051

Australia

Greenpeace Australia
PO Box 800
Surry Hills
NSW 2010
Tel: +61 2 9211 4066

Friends of the Earth
134 Broadway
NSW 2007
Tel: +61 2 9283 2004

Canada

Greenpeace Canada
250 Dundas St W
Suite 605
Toronto, Ont. M5T 2Z5
Tel: +1 416 597 8408
Fax: +1 416 597 8422
Website:
www.greenpeacecanada.org

The Sierra Club
Coordinates the Canadian Climate
Action Network of over a hundred
groups.
Suite 412
1 Nicholas St
Ottawa, Ont K1B 7B7
Tel: +1 888 810 4204
Fax: +1 613 241 2292
E-mail: Sierra@web.net
Website: www.sierraclub.ca

The Pembina Insitute
Specializes in energy and air issues.
124 O'Conner St
Suite 505
Ottawa, Ont. K1P 5M9
Tel: +1 613 235 6288
Fax: +1 613 235 8118
Website: www.pembina.org
Their climate solutions website is at
www.climatechangesolutions.com

UK

Greenpeace UK
Canonbury Villas
London N1 2PN
Tel: +44 20 7865 8100
Fax: +44 20 7865 8200
E-mail: info@uk.greenpeace.org
Website: greenpeace.org/-
uk/science

Friends of the Earth UK
Energy Campaign
26-28 Underwood Street
London N1 7JQ
Tel: +44 20 7490 1555
Fax: +44 20 7490 0881
E-mail: padg@foe.co.uk
Website: www.foe.org

USA

Greenpeace USA
702 H Street
Washington, DC 20001
Tel: +1 800 326 0959

US Climate Action Network
The US branch of a worldwide
network that works to inform and
influence US and international
policies.
1367 Connecticut Ave, NW
Suite 300
Washington, DC 20036
Tel: +1 202 785 8702
Fax: +1 202 785 8701
E-mail: cielne@igc.org
Website:
www.climatenetwork.org/USCAN/ab
out.html

Worldwatch Institute
1776 Massachusetts Ave, NW
Washington, D.C. 20036-1904
Tel: +1 202 452 1999
Fax: +1 202 296 7365
E-mail: worldwatch@worldwatch.org
Website: www.worldwatch.org

Bibliography

Books

The Breakdown of Climate: Human Choices or Global Disaster?, Peter Bunyard (Floris Books, Edinburgh, 1999).

The Carbon War: Dispatches from the End of the Oil Century, Jeremy Leggett (Allen Lane/Penguin, London, 1999).

Catastrophe: An Investigation into the Origins of the Modern World, David Keys (Arrow Books, London, 2000; Random House, New York, 1999).

Factor Four: Doubling Wealth, Halving Resource Use, Ernst von Weizsäcker, Amory B Lovins and L Hunter Lovins (Earthscan, London, 1998).

Fair Weather? Equity Concerns in Climate Change, Ed. Ferenc L Tóth (Earthscan, London, 1999).

Global Environmental Change: Plants, Animals and Communities, Jonathan Graves and Duncan Riley (Longman, Harlow, 1996).

Greening the North: A Post-Industrial Blueprint for Ecology and Equity, Wolfgang Sachs, Reinhard Loske, Manfred Linz et al (Zed Books, London and New York, 1998).

Health and Climate Change: Modelling the Impacts of Global Warming and Ozone Depletion, Pim Martens (Earthscan, London, 1998).

The Heat is On: The Climate Crisis, the Cover Up, the Prescription, Ross Gelbspan (Perseus Books, Reading, Massachusetts, 1998).

The Planetary Interest, Ed. Kennedy Graham (UCL Press, London, 1999).

Playing Safe: Science and the Environment, Jonathon Porritt (Thames and Hudson, London, 2000).

Sharing the World: Sustainable Living and Global Equity in the 21st Century, Michael Carley and Philippe Spapens (Earthscan, London, 1998).

Periodicals

Down to Earth	*New Scientist*
The Ecologist	*Science*
Nature	*The New Internationalist* **www.newint.org**

Additional internet resources

www.climatevoice.org – Tell world leaders that you want action on climate change through this campaigning site.

www.cru.uea.ac.uk/link – Original research and news, created by the Climatic Research Unit of the University of East Anglia.

www.epa.gov/globalwarming – The US Environmental Protection Agency.

www.heatisonline.org – Ross Gelbspan's (see above) updates on extreme weather worldwide. Excellent.

www.met-office.gov.uk/research/hadleycentre/index.html – The UK's Hadley Center for Climate Prediction and Research.

www.ncdc.noaa.gov – The US National Climatic Data Center's archive of weather data.

www.oneworld.org/cse/index.html – The Delhi-based Center for Science and Environment's site with information from a Southern perspective.

www.seen.org – The Sustainable Energy and Economy Network's exhaustive reports on the World Bank's funding of fossil-fuel projects.

Index

Index